A HISTORY OF DIDSBURY

A
HISTORY OF
DIDSBURY

BY

IVOR R. MILLION LL.B

FOREWORD BY
LADY SIMON OF WYTHENSHAWE

PUBLISHED JOINTLY BY
DIDSBURY CIVIC SOCIETY & E. J. MORTEN (Publishers)
DIDSBURY, MANCHESTER
1969

FIRST PUBLISHED 1969

© 1969 DIDSBURY CIVIC SOCIETY

SBN 901598 00 3

REPRINTED JULY 1969

DESIGN AND LAYOUT BY RONDO PUBLICATIONS LTD.

PRINTED BY THE ACORN PRESS LTD, 10 PALL MALL, LIVERPOOL.

FOREWORD

I feel it an honour to be asked to write a Foreword to this book—'A History of Didsbury'. Mr. Million's work illuminates many details of Didsbury's past as it is unfolded through the centuries. He has produced a most worthy successor to the books of Alderman Fletcher Moss, on which we have relied for some aspects of Didsbury's history for so long.

Most of us whose school days are far behind think of history as lists of dates—Kings, Queens and battles fought far from these shores; but the modern child finds that history is much more interesting. It is something which is being made all the time, and we are all part of it. Residents of Didsbury who read this book will find that highways leading now to central Manchester—such as Wilmslow Road—were not so long ago, tracks through cultivated fields and farms, all with their names collected from old documents by Mr. Million. Chapters Six and Seven give an imaginary walk in Didsbury by an inhabitant of the eighteenth century.

Here is an account of all the changes which led to the building of houses, shops, schools and Churches, for the population grew particularly rapidly after the arrival of the railway in 1879. It is fascinating to wonder what a future citizen of the year 2000 would find if he compared his environment with what we know to-day.

I hope future local historians will be inspired by Mr. Million's work to find answers to questions which even he leaves alone. But in many respects this new book promises and deserves to be a standard work of local history. It will be of permanent value to Didsbury and to all those who are and will be interested in this place, and how it came to be as it is.

Shena D. Simon
(Lady Simon of Wythenshawe.)

PREFACE

During the winter of 1967 I delivered a lecture to the Historical Section oi the Didsbury Civic Society on the feudal system in Didsbury, after which several members asked me to commit what I had said to writing. This I agreed to do but, on considering the matter further, it occurred to me that the time was ripe for a new book dealing with all aspects of Didsbury's history. This was in no way to decry the earlier historians of the district, Rev. John Booker and Alderman Fletcher Moss, but since their works were produced the Lancashire County Record Office has been opened, the families of de Trafford, Egerton of Tatton and Tatton of Wythenshawe have placed their private documents on view to the general public, the records of Parliament have been made available to anyone wishing to see them; the admirable indexes prepared by the Record Society of Lancashire & Cheshire have appeared in print and, in very recent years, the technique of photocopying has been developed and perfected. The result of these changes has been that I have been able, in the comfort of my own home, to peruse photocopies of documents of which neither Booker or Moss had ever heard and to which they could never have had sufficient access even if it had been otherwise. I have endeavoured to supplement their work, not to replace it. That is why so little appears here about the history of St. James's Church. I could not hope to improve on what they wrote on that subject.

Even before I conceived the idea of writing the book Mr. Ernest France readily placed the fruits of his own researches at my disposal and I have benefitted greatly from comparing notes and ideas with him about each fragment of material that either of us has discovered. I have been flattered indeed by the interest and encouragement shown to me by Mr. N. J. Frangopulo, head of the Department of Historical Studies at Didsbury College of Education, who has not only read the manuscript and acted as the candid friend who is such an asset to any author but also, in company with Mr. John Duke, Mr. J. G. Mackley, and Mr. C. Wolfson, has attended to some of the business aspects of producing the book. I have received enormous assistance from the staffs of the British Museum, the Public Record Office, the House of Lords Record Office, the Manchester Central Library, John Rylands Library and the Lancashire County Record Office. Nevertheless some of the photocopies which I obtained from these places would have been useless to me had it not been for the help I received from Dr. J. H. Denton, of Manchester University, who very kindly transcribed a number of mediaeval documents which were incomprehensible to my untrained eyes. I am nost grateful also to Mr. Maurice Brunner who went through the manuscript sentence by sentence and rectified the grosser infelicities of my grammar and style.

My debt to the Didsbury Civic Society and Messrs. Eric J. Morten who, in conjunction, have published the work is too obvious to require explanation and I count myself as fortunate indeed that so distinguished a resident of Didsbury as Lady Simon of Wythenshawe agreed to write the Foreword. I must also acknowledge the help I have received from the many people, too numerous to list, who have allowed me to see documents in their possession or have helped me with their reminiscences or advice. They include a Peer, a Peeress, a member of the Privy Council and a Professor of the Hebrew University of Jerusalem.

I thank them all. Lastly I wish to pay a tribute to my wife; poor recompense indeed for the many long hours during which she has heard nothing from my direction except the scratching of a pen.

Ivor R. Million

March, 1969

CONTENTS

LIST OF ILLUSTRATIONS

Chapter I

THE HISTORY OF THE MANOR

The hamlet of Didsbury was never a manor in its own right, although for some reason it was described as such in a few seventeenth and eighteenth century documents. For instance a deed dated in 1752, whereby the lord of the manor, Sir John Bland, mortgaged his estates referred to the "manor or lordship or reputed manor or lordship of Didsbury". Indeed it was not uncommon for a hamlet to be described in this way. There also exists a deed, dated 1636, which referred to the "manor or Lordshippe of Lansham als Levenshulme", and all the deeds of the estate appurtenant to Barlow Hall, Chorlton-cum-Hardy, referred to the Manor of Barlow. The truth of the matter is that these places were all parts of the Manor of Withington.

Although manors are commonly thought of as confined to the mediaeval era they were never formally abolished. Until quite recent times their institutions survived. Accordingly, in tracing the history and institutions of the Manor of Withington, we must draw from all periods.

According to modern terminology the Manor of Withington included (or should we say includes?) Withington, Didsbury, Chorlton-cum-Hardy, Burnage, Rusholme, Levenshulme and Moss Side in a continuous land block, with Denton and Haughton as a detached part. There is also evidence that Anglezark and Longworth, both in the Parish of Bolton, were parts of the same manor. The inquisition post mortem of Christopher Longworth, who died in 1608, mentioned that he held lands in Longworth of Rowland Mosley as of his Manor of Withington, and the attendance register of the Manorial Court showed that in 1734 one Henry Hutton attended for "lands lying in Longworth in the Parish of Bolton".

The position which the manor held can only be understood by reference to the feudal system as a whole. We must start with the Norman Conquest, when as rewards for help in conquering England, William the Conqueror divided the country between a large number of his supporters.

11

In most cases they were obliged, in return, to supply him with a certain number of armed knights, that being his method of ensuring the availability of an army, but in other cases they rendered different services, such as bearing the regalia on ceremonial occasions, carrying his arms in battle, or even praying for his soul.

In the case of Lancashire, William granted it to Roger of Poitou, from whom it was confiscated very shortly afterwards, and in the Domesday Book we read:-

> "King William holds all the land between the Ribble and the Mersey which Roger of Poitou held".

Unfortunately the book contains no record of the services which Roger rendered for these lands.

The lands granted by William to his immediate subordinates were, of course, far too extensive for them to cultivate themselves. Consequently they, in their turn, parcelled them out between subordinates of their own in return for similar services as they themselves rendered to the King. In this way Albert Grelley became lord of the Barony of Manchester, which included a number of manors in various parts of Lancashire, the chief of which was the Manor of Manchester itself. This was bounded by the Irwell, the Mersey and the Tame. As regards the services which Grelley and his successors rendered we are told in a Survey made in 1322:-

> "The Manor of Manchester is held from Thomas Earl of Lancaster for 5¼ knights' fees paying yearly 52s 6d at St. John the Baptist and £4. 2. 6d. for sak-fee at the four terms."

A knight's fee was the obligation of supplying one fully armed knight for forty days a year. Originally the obligations were required to be taken literally, but at a very early stage they were commuted for money payments. It was this which made possible the existence of a fraction of a knight's fee.

Subordinate to the Manor of Manchester were three sub-manors, Ashton-under-Lyne, Withington and Heaton Norris. The service rendered by the Lord of the Manor of Withington was one knight's fee, to which many references exist in various documents. At some time prior to 1320 this was commuted to a money payment, for in the Survey of 1320 (There were surveys in both 1320 and 1322) we are told:-

> "Nicholas de Longforde, for one fee in Wythington, homage fealty and suit of court, worth 6s 8d, paying for sake 9s and for ward 10s and putary serjeant and arms or armour."

The payments totalling 19/- were made unvaried for many a long year. In the rent book of the Manor of Manchester for 1474, when the lord of the Manor again bore the name Nicholas Longford we read:-

> "Nick Langforth miles tenet   IXs et p
> dmd de Withington et Didsbury   Ward castr
> y suit I feod milite de dic   Xs"
> dno et r p Anne

Similarly in the rent book of 1592:-

| "Nicholas Longfforde ar | Of hym for one wholle yeares cheiffe Rente then due for the hamell of Withington whereof be members didysburye houghe Barlowe, hardye, half chorleton mosse syde Rushehulme & Denton with th' appurtenances" | XIXs |

In 1596 Nicholas Mosley, a former Lord Mayor of London, purchased the Manor of Manchester, and when, in the following year, his son, Rowland Mosley purchased the sub-manor of Withington the manor and sub-manor were owned by father and son respectively. It would seem that at that stage the payment of the rent of 19/- fell into disuse. Nicholas Mosley died in 1612, and the Manor of Manchester was inherited by his son, which meant, of course, that he was lord of both the manor and the sub-manor.

The first reference to the Manor of Withington appears to have been contained in the Great Inquest of lands given and made within the County of Lancaster, which was made in June 1212.

"Mahthew (sic) son of William, and Roger, son of William, hold the fee of one knight of Robert Gredle in Withington of ancient time, and must find a judge for the King."

It is not known when Withington came into existence as a separate manor, but its obligation to find a judge for the King suggests that it possibly dates back to the Saxon era. The King was lord of the Manor of Salford in Saxon times. The direct duty owned to him by the Manor of Withington leads us to think that it was a manor in its own right even before Manchester, which must have been imposed above it.

In addition to the knight's fee it appears that the lord of the Manor of Withington was obliged to supply agricultural services as well, for the inquisition post mortem of Robert Grelley, taken in 1282, stated:-

"There is a certain fee of Wythington which owes yearly a certain ploughing of 15 acres of land, which is worth 7s 6d yearly; and a certain custom from the said fee to reap in autumn, pertaining to 30 levates of land, which is worth 2s 6d yearly."

In addition the lord of the Manor of Withington was obliged to do suit and service at the manorial court of Manchester, the Court Leet as it was called. Once again, we turn to the inquisition post mortem of Robert Grelley:-

"John de Birum holds Wytington for the term of his life for the fee of one knight and does suit to the court of the barony (or court baron) of Mamecestre from three weeks to three weeks."

Since the lord of the Manor of Withington was one of the tenants of the

13

Manor of Manchester, changes in the ownership of Withington were noted by the Manchester Court Leet and entered in its records. At its session on 2nd October, 1595, it was recorded:-

> "The Jurye dothe presente that Nicholas Longforde esquier hath soulde to the Ho: Sir Roberte Cycell knighte to Mr. Hygh Byston esquier et als, the Lordshippe of Withington, and that ye sayde Sr Roberte Cicell Etc the sayde Hughe Byston et alls are to come and doe theire suite and service."

Having discussed the relationship between the lord of the Manor of Withington and those above him let us examine the position with regard to those below him.

At a very early stage the lords sold considerable areas of the manor to free tenants. The archives of the de Trafford family, now happily preserved at the Lancashire County Record Office in Preston, include superb examples of the deeds whereby this was done.

> "Know all men, present and future, that I Matthew de Hathersage have given conceded and by this my present charter have confirmed to Richard de Trafford and his heirs in return for homage and service all the land that Adam the son of Alexander de Diddesbury held of me for the term of his life within these boundaries beginning at Cringlebrook and so following the ditch towards the north as far as Holdholmbrook and so following Holdholmbrook as far as the boundary which is between Richard de Trafford's land and Thermannes Croft and from there towards the west as far as the highway and so following the highway as far as Holdholmbrook and so following the ditch of Holdholmbrook towards the south to Cringlebrook and so following Cringlebrook as far as the said ditch and the common of pasture in Withington wherein my free tenants of Withington participate To Have and To Hold the same of me ánd my heirs to him and his heirs except Jews and ecclesiastics freely quietly peacefully and unharmed rendering for the same to me and my heirs annually two silver shillings at the feast of Saint Michael and the Annunciation of Blessed Mary."

The important words in this deed were the words "To Have and To Hold the same of me and my heirs", for although the land was granted to Richard de Trafford he held it under Matthew de Hathersage as lord of the manor. Nothing was said about feudal services but we may rest assured that they existed. They were referred to in land transfers even centuries later. In 1682 the then lord of the manor, Sir Edward Mosley, sold land which is now part of Fog Lane Park to William Birch under payment of a chief or quit rent of 7/9d which was for performance of suit and service to the Manor of Withington, and as late as 1885 we find Lord Egerton of Tatton leasing land, now part of Hough End Playing Fields, to Henry Shaw Holford, "he paying the sum of 10/6d upon the death of each and every person dying principal tenant of the said demised premises or any part thereof for and in the name of an heriot and likewise doing and performing suit and service to and at the Court Leet and at the Court Baron which shall from time to time be held and kept in and the Manor of Withington aforesaid". People are living today who were living when that lease was granted.

Although many of the place-names in the deed whereby Matthew de Hathersage granted his land to Richard de Trafford are now quite meaningless, the land it referred to can nevertheless be identified. The Cringle Brook still forms the northern boundary of Burnage. It gives its name to Cringle Hall Road. Flowing in a westerly direction it passes under Wilmslow Road near Brook Road, to which it also gives its name. The highway was almost certainly the road which we now know as Wilmslow Road, although we cannot rule out the possibility that it was Burnage Lane. Accordingly the land was probably that part of Fallowfield lying to the north of Brook Road on the easterly side of Wilmslow Road. On the other hand, if the highway was Burnage Lane, then it was in the neighbourhood of the Duchess of York Hospital for Babies.

The reference to Jews is full of interest. There is no evidence that Jews lived in the Manchester area at any time prior to about 1770. While at first sight the deed appears to afford such evidence the prohibition it contained was quite common in deeds of land in all parts of the country. However, they help us to determine the date of the deed. It must have been executed before 1290, when the Jews were expelled from England by Edward I. In point of fact the prohibition against ecclesiastics shows that it antedated the Statute of Mortmain, 1224.

Apart from the de Trafford muniments we have some few further records of the tenures under which parts of the manor were sold off. The inquisition post mortem of George Birch of Birch Hall, which stood where Manchester Grammar School stands now, is one of them. At his death in 1611 he held Birch Hall and about 130 Lancashire acres in Birch and Rusholme by the 50th part of a knight's fee and 2d rent. One of his ancestors appears to have purchased about half of this in 1323 from Nicholas Longford, who was then lord of the manor. The inquisition post mortem of Sir Alexander Barlow, who died in 1620, noted that he held Barlow Hall and its lands of Edward Mosley, lord of the manor, in free socage by fealty and the yearly rent of 20d. Socage, it should be explained, was the obligation to render agricultural services. On the other hand the pleadings in a law suit, brought in 1600 by Edward Mosley's father, Rowland Mosley, against the same Sir Alexander Barlow stated that he held his estates "by Knightes service and by a certayne yearlye Rente as a Charterer and freeholder of the said Mannor of Withington". In all probability the pleadings were correct. Rowland Mosley could be expected to know the truth of the matter whereas inquisitions post mortem were frequently inaccurate.

Very little indeed is known of any early land transfers in Didsbury except that in 1341 Thomas de Bruche of Diddesbury sold 14 acres to Roger de Barlowe and Ellen, his wife, for 10 marks. We do not know where this land was although the fact that the purchasers were the owners of Barlow Hall suggests that it lay in that direction. We know of no other sale until 1539, when Ralph Longford sold to Robert Tatton an island in the Mersey, known as the Myddope, then part of Didsbury but now part of Northenden. It lay near the old mill in Mill Lane, Northenden, and has now been joined to the south bank of the river. In 1546 John Byrom sold upwards of 24 Lancashire acres in the area to Ralph Pycrofte.

The Manor of Withington was governed by its own court, the Court Leet and Great Court Baron held at Withington. This is said to have met, during the eighteenth and nineteenth centuries, at the Red Lion Hotel. It met twice a year at the end of April and October or the beginning of May and November. Although the records of the Manchester Court Leet, dating from 1552, are still in existence, those of the Withington Court Leet cannot, alas, be traced, although it is known to have existed from the thirteenth century. All that remains is the suit roll, or attendance register, for the session which took place on 29th April, 1734. For some unexplained reason this found its way into the possession of the churchwardens of St. James's Church, who preserved it.

The only fragment of a record which we have of the actual proceedings of the court is contained in the books of Thomas Wood, landlord of the Ring o'Bells Inn at the commencement of the nineteenth century.

"1803   Expences about Jno Howard's Ditches and
Nov 4   other persons being measured to be presented   9. 1.
Nov 7   Other Expences when presented this
         day Walner's Lane 630 Yds. Famous
         Pits 68 Yds   1. 11.
                                                             11. 0.
   7   Expences at Withington Court   10. 6.
   7   Lent James Wood Clark at Withington   1. 0.
   7   Presented John Howard's Ditches in
         Walmer Lane 630 Yds in Famous Pits Field
         68 Yds at Withington Court, allowed till
         the 1st of January 1804 to do them".

As Thomas Wood was himself the tenant of Famous Pits Field, which lay on Parrs Wood Lane where the allotments now are, he was presumably prosecuting a neighbour for blocking the ditches. Walmer's (or Warner's) Lane was the path which, even today runs beside the railway line as far as Parrs Wood Road.

With the passing of the Public Health Act, 1872, and the creation of the Withington Local Board of Health the Court Leet lost nearly all its functions, but it seems to have carried on at least until 1885, after which it died a natural death. In its last years it is said that those present sat down to a joyous dinner after the sitting.

As we do not know when the Manor of Withington came into existence it is not possible to say who its first lord was. It may have been William, son of Wulfrith de Withington, who, at some date prior to 1212, was involved in a dispute with Gospatric de Chorlton about the ownership of

16

land in Chorlton. The dispute was settled by wager of battle, as was not uncommon at that time. Gospatric appointed his brother, Adam, to fight as his champion, as a reward for which he gave him one eighth of Chorlton. In the event the battle was won by William.

William's sons were Matthew and Roger. Matthew can almost certainly be identified with Matthew de Hathersage. We do not know which of the two brothers died first but in 1224 we find that the lord of the manor was Matthew, son of Matthew de Hathersage, who presumably inherited it from his father. He still owned the manor in 1242. It was probably he who sold the land near Cringlebrook to Richard de Trafford.

The younger Matthew de Hathersage had two daughters, Cecilia, who married Nigel de Longford, and another daughter who married Gousil de Barlborough, who was probably also known as Simon de Gousil. At this period it is difficult to determine exactly who the lord of the manor was. The Lancashire Assize Rolls name Simon de Gousil and John de Byrom as joint lords in 1276 and 1278, yet, as we have seen, the inquisition post mortem of Robert Grelley, taken in 1282, mentioned that John de Byrom held the manor for the term of his life. To add to the confusion there are deeds which suggest that Simon de Gousil alone was the lord.

The next lord of the manor was probably Sir John Longford. We cannot determine how he came to inherit it. It was in one of two possible ways. He was the grandson of Nigel de Longford, who married Cecilia de Hathersage and also, as an infant, he was a ward of Sir John de Byrom, whose daughter, Joan, he married. He fought with Edward I in Flanders and fought also against William Wallace at Falkirk.

The Longford family held the Manor of Withington until 1593. They were very typical of the titled families of their day. They thought more of fighting than of improving their landed holdings and one or other of them was present at many of the famous battles at which English troops fought in the Middle Ages.

Sir Nicholas de Longford, son of Sir John, was one of the knights who joined the rebellion of the Earl of Lancaster which was crushed by Edward II in 1322 at the Battle of Boroughbridge where he was taken prisoner. After the battle a party of men from Cheshire, loyal to the King, and under the command of one Oliver de Ingham, crossed the Mersey at Stretford, ostensibly to intercept the rebels fleeing from the battlefield, but eager for plunder they fanned out and ravaged villages as far apart as Urmston, Bury and Heaton Norris. Taking advantage of the absence of Sir Nicholas, they came to his manor house at Withington where they stole a number of farm animals and various implements, but the fact that almost everything they took was for outdoor use leads us to think that they failed to get into the manor house itself.

Sir Nicholas was eventually pardoned for his part in the rebellion and was later present at both the Battle of Crecy and the Siege of Calais.

Another Sir Nicholas Longford, who was lord of the manor, was killed at the Battle of Shrewsbury in 1403 and yet another fought at Agincourt in 1415 at the head of 500 archers.

At the death of this last named Sir Nicholas two inquisitions post mortem were taken. The first mentioned that he died possessed of the Manor of Withington which he held of Thomas la Warre, lord of the Manor of Manchester, while the second, taken nine weeks later, stated that he held the manor directly from the King. The explanation of this second inquisition, which was completely contrary to the facts, was that Sir John de Stanley pretended to discover that the manor was held directly of the King but that that fact had previously been concealed. As a reward for his diligence in making this astounding discovery, Henry V committed the custody of the manor to him, subject to certain rights in favour of Sir Nicholas's relatives, until Ralph Longford, the rightful owner, and a ward of Sir John de Stanley, should attain his majority.

Thus, by flagrant collusion between his guardian and his sovereign, Ralph Longford, a lad of 15, was cheated of his birthright for six years. Even so he was more fortunate than Thomas la Warre, who was stripped of his rights completely, a state of affairs which, in his case, was apparently intended to be permanent. For how long the sovereign usurped the payments due to the lord of the Manor of Manchester we do not know, but by 1431 they had been restored.

Ralph Longford was knighted at the Battle of Vermeuil in 1431. On his death the manor came into the hands of his son, yet another Sir Nicholas.

Nothing is known of the doings of this Sir Nicholas prior to 1470, on which date the Sheriff of Derby was instructed to arrest him for treason. Hearing of this Sir Nicholas went into hiding at the manor house at Withington where Christopher Langton, one of the sheriff's officers, came to apprehend him but left hurriedly in the face of threats on his life by Longford's servant. He returned next day and placed the Privy Seal letter on a seat near the door of the house. Sir Nicholas, however, had not been idle in the meantime and had collected and armed twenty servants who, under the command of his nephew, John Longford, pursued Longton to the gates of the demesne, where they overtook him. After beating him and endeavouring to push the Privy Seal letter down his throat they took him back to the manor house where they put him in the stocks. They then took him to Poynton and eventually he was conveyed to Longford itself, in Derbyshire, where he was imprisoned.

The King again ordered the Sheriff of Derby to arrest Sir Nicholas. We do not know the outcome, but the fact that his son, yet again a Nicholas, had succeeded him by the following year, suggests that his politics and his bravado cost him his life.

The new lord of the manor was knighted at the Battle of Tewkesbury in 1471 and is said to have died in Scotland in 1482.

His brother, Ralph Longford, who succeeded him, was to have been knighted at the coronation of Edward V, one of the ill-fated princes in the Tower, but that coronation never took place and he had to wait for his knighthood until the Battle of Stoke in 1487.

Ralph Longford's son, Nicholas, predeceased him and the next lord of the manor was his grandson, also named Ralph Longford, who was knighted in 1533 at the coronation of Anne Boleyn. As we shall see it was he who entered into agreements with Robert Tatton about a ferry boat on the River Mersey. He seems to have frequented the royal court where his extravagance got him into difficulties, for in 1543 we find him in the Fleet Prison because of a debt owed to the King. While there he made desperate attempts to dispose of the Manor of Withington to Sir John Gates, a privy chamberlain. At some stage he appears to have borrowed £3,000 from Gates and eventually he entered into a contract to sell the Manor of Withington to him for £650, the debt to be cancelled at the same time, but for some reason this contract was never put into effect.

The last Longford to own the manor was Sir Nicholas Longford. By his time the financial difficulties of the family had reached such proportions that he was obliged to sell it. This he did on 30th July, 1593, for £2,100 to Sir Robert Cecil, Hugh Beeston, Michael Hicks and Humphrey Flint.

Much has been written elsewhere of Sir Robert Cecil, the Elizabethan statesman through whose efforts James I was brought to the throne of England, but of his three associates nothing is known, although they may, in some way, have been nominees of the Crown, the sixteenth century equivalent of Crown Estate Commissioners. They held the manor for only four years, disposing of it on 13th December, 1597, to Rowland Mosley whose residence was Hough End Hall. After the sale Sir Nicholas Mosley represented his son in the ceremonies whereby it was publicly announced in the district that the manor had a new lord. After Sir Nicholas's death in 1612 the Mosley freize, which can still be seen in St. James's Church, was erected.

Rowland Mosley survived his father for only four years. His son, Edward, was still a baby when he died. Possibly due to the absence of a father's influence he developed dissolute habits and it was deemed advisable to arrange a marriage for him at an early age. He strongly supported Charles I from whom he received a baronetcy in 1640. During the Civil War he is said to have raised troops from his Lancashire estates, which included Withington. He was taken prisoner by the Parliamentarians at Middlewich in 1643 but was released against a promise not to bear arms for the King again. After the war his estates were confiscated by the victorious Parliament, but he was allowed to redeem them on payment of a fine of £4,874. He died at Hough End in 1657, being succeeded by his son, Edward, a boy of 18.

The second Sir Edward was a man of very feeble constitution. He died on 14th October, 1665, in his 28th year. It was he who, as we shall see, endowed Didsbury's first school.

He was succeeded as lord of the manor by his cousin, Edward Mosley, who, coming as he did from a different branch of the family, lived at Hulme Hall, Hulme. He was a lawyer of some attainment, eventually becoming a judge. Unlike his predecessors, who had espoused the Stuart cause, he appears to have been in favour of the revolution of 1688 as a result of which he was knighted in 1689. He died in 1693.

The only child of his who survived him was his daughter Ann, who was married in 1685, at Chorlton Chapel, to Sir John Bland of Kippax Hall, Yorkshire, who sat in Parliament, first for Appleby and later for Pontefract. By his Will Sir Edward left the Manor of Withington to Sir John and Lady Ann Bland jointly. Despite his membership of the House of Commons, Sir John's main interest was not politics but gambling, an occupation which he carried on with total disregard for the welfare either of his family or of his estate. He died on 25th October, 1715, and was buried at Didsbury where the wall plaque, erected to his memory, can still be seen.

Lady Ann Bland survived until 26th July, 1734. She it was who led the break-away from the Collegiate Church in Manchester to found St. Ann's Church, which was named after her. There is a monument to her, also, in St. James's Church.

Her son, the second Sir John Bland, inherited the Manor of Withington from her. He too sat in Parliament. In 1715 he was indicted for treason and, while no details of the alleged offence are known, one cannot help observing that that was the year of the Old Pretender's insurrection. Perhaps Sir John was accused of giving him assistance. In any event, he seems to have been acquitted, for he survived to tell the tale until 14th April, 1742, when he died at Bath.

The third Sir John Bland, who was his son, inherited his grandfather's vices. By 1752, he appears to have been in grave financial difficulties. On 30th June of that year he mortgaged the manor and a great deal of land in the township of Withington to William Fenwick of Bywell, Northumberland, for £5,000. On the same day he also mortgaged land in Didsbury to Joshua Cox of Holborn for £8,000 and the Manor of Cheadle Hulme, which he also owned, to Richard Shelley of St. George's, Hanover Square, for £3,000. Thus, in one day, he borrowed £16,000, a great sum in modern times, an astronomical figure two hundred years ago. Nor did these loans see the end of his difficulties. On 28th June, 1753, he borrowed a further £2,000 from William Fenwick and on 20th December in the same year a further £2,000 from the same source.

Clearly Sir John was well set on the road to ruin. The only remedy was to sell up his estates and indeed he had embarked on this expedient by the beginning of 1753. The chief purchasers of his lands in Withington and Didsbury were the Broome family.

The Manor of Withington was purchased by Samuel Egerton of Tatton Park, but as the deed whereby it was conveyed to him has been lost, we do not know the date of the transaction. Sir John Bland died on 3rd September, 1755, and it may be that for a short time, until the sale to Samuel Egerton, the lord of the manor was his brother, Sir Hungerford Bland. What we do know is that it was not until 1758 that Samuel Egerton purchased a large holding of land in Withington, as distinct from the lordship of the manor.

Samuel Egerton died in 1780. His estates were inherited by his sister, Hester, who was the wife of William Tatton of Wythenshawe Hall. Thus Withington acquired its second female lord of the manor. She lies buried in St. Wilfrid's Church, Northenden. On inheriting her brother's estate she changed her surname back to Egerton, possibly in pusuance of a requirement to that effect in his will. She held the manor for only a very short time, dying in the same year as her brother.

William Egerton, her son, inherited the manor from her. He started to erect the present Tatton Hall, but he died in 1806, before it was completed.

His son, Wilbraham Egerton, succeeded him. He died in 1856. He, in his turn, was succeeded by his son, William Tatton Egerton, who was Member of Parliament for Cheshire. In 1859, he was created Baron Egerton of Tatton. He died in 1883 and was succeeded by his son, Wilbraham Egerton, who was created Earl Egerton and Viscount Salford in 1897. Wilbraham Road, Fallowfield, was, of course, named after him. Earl Egerton of Tatton was chairman of the Manchester Ship Canal Company at the time the canal was dug and in fact he himself cut the first sod in 1887.

It was at just about this time that Withington began to feel the full impact of the spread of population from Manchester. Little by little, the Egerton lands were bought up, mainly for ribbon development along Wilmslow Road, but the Egertons kept strict control over the land even after they had sold it. A chief rent was reserved on each sale and stringent conditions written into the title deeds. In particular, shops and business premises were not permitted to be built where they had not been built before. That is why there are no shops or business premises between Fallowfield and Withington.

Earl Egerton died in 1909 and since he had no son the earldom became extinct, but his younger brother, the Hon. Alan de Tatton Egerton succeeded him as Baron Egerton. He died in 1920 and his son, the Hon. Maurice Egerton, succeeded him as the fourth and last Baron Egerton of Tatton. He was an adventurer indeed. He held Certificate No.11 of the Royal Aero Club and was a pioneer of motoring and wireless transmission. He was a much-travelled man and at Tatton Park there is a magnificent exhibition of his sporting trophies. He died, unmarried, in 1958, and the barony became extinct. All the lands in South Manchester, formerly belonging to the Egerton family, have now been sold, but technically the lordship of the Manor of Withington still belongs to the executors of the fourth baron.

Chapter II

THE APPEARANCE OF THE MANOR

Before endeavouring to assess the appearance of Didsbury in the Middle Ages let us describe a typical mediaeval manor.

At the focal point would be the manor house which would normally be a fortified structure surrounded by a moat. Surrounding the manor house would be the demesne of the lord of the manor in which lay his land, farms and private grounds. Lying outside the demesne there would, of course, be a village, or if the manor was a large one, several villages. In the immediate vicinity of the village would be two or three large fields divided into strips known as doles, each approximately 16½ feet wide. These were distributed among the villagers by lot, each man being the tenant of about a dozen strips scattered about each of the fields. As every school child knows the fields grew wheat and barley and lay fallow in rotation. Beyond the fields would lie the common on which the villagers had the right to pasture their animals. In the centre of the village would be a village green, around which would stand cottages. There would, of course, be a church, although in the north of England, where the manors were very large and the country sparsely populated, each church would serve a number of villages. There would also be a mill, belonging to the lord of the manor, where the villagers ground their corn and paid the lord a toll for so doing. If the manor stood on a river the mill would stand at the water's edge and be worked by water power. In the age which we are now considering the population was so small that, even with the wasteful agricultural methods in use, only a fraction of the country's land resources were utilized. Consequently, the land between one village and another would be in its natural uncultivated state. This was the manorial waste.

Although Hough End Hall must in later years have competed with Barlow Hall for the honour of being considered the most grandiose residence in the district the mediaeval manor house did not stand on that site. The earliest date to which the history of Hough End can be traced is

1465 when it is said to have been the home of Jenkyn Mosley, an ancestor of the family which we have already noted. The manor house was a building known as the Hough, lying where Mauldeth Road now crosses Princess Parkway. Around the house was a moat which, to this day, gives its name to Old Moat Lane. The house is said to have survived until the eighteenth century, when it was replaced by another structure. At that time it was known as Old Hall Farm. The moat, or at least a portion of it, survived into the twentieth century when it was filled in and the manor house demolished to make room for the Manchester Corporation housing estate. If the reader would wish to trace the site of the Hough he should go to Eddisbury Avenue behind Mauldeth Road. Here on the wall of a short terrace of houses he will see a magnificent bronze plaque inscribed as follows:-

"This tablet recalls the completion of 10,000 houses built by the Corporation of Manchester to house the working-classes of the City between the years 1919 to 1928. The group of houses to which this tablet is attached stands upon the land originally enclosed by the moat of the ancient manor house of Withington; the arms of four of the lords of the manor who held their lands in succession under the barony of Manchester being reproduced on this tablet.

Unveiled September 6th 1928."

In the four corners of the plaque are the arms of the Hathersage, Longford, Mosley and Egerton families. Worked into the bronze at the foot is a plan of the housing estate superimposed on a plan of the old hall and the moat.

We are able to trace the boundaries of the lord's demesne with precision. They are shown on the Tithe Map of 1845, and indeed there exists, among the Egerton of Tatton documents, an undated map of the demesne which appears to have been drawn at the end of the eighteenth century, or possibly the beginning of the nineteenth. It included places as far apart as the sites of Whalley Range, Alexandra Park, Platt Lane Police Station, Old Moat Senior School, Withington Hospital, Hough End Playing Fields, Chorlton Park and Hough End Hall.

The origins of the demesne are shrouded in mystery but some evidence of its age can be deduced from the Schedule to the Tithe Map, which recited that the demesne, which comprised 1,195 acres, was covered from the payment of tithes in kind by the payment of the annual sum of £1.16.8d to the Dean and Canons of Manchester in lieu thereof. In view of the fact that the tithes payable in 1845 from the 2,501 acres of the Township of Withington amounted to £135.9.0d it will readily be appreciated that the 1,195 acres in the demesne must have been assessed for £1.16.8d in an age when money values were radically different from what they were in 1845. In fact it seems clear that the boundaries were settled in the Middle Ages.

The first clear reference to the demesne which has come down to us appears to be in the Survey of 1322. This stated the boundary of the Manor of Manchester, which included the Manor of Withington, as following the Melschelache "unto Wythinton Howe (i.e. Hough) and from thence following between Wythinton Howe and Trafford unto the bounds of Chorlerton (Chorlton)". This referred to that portion of the boundary of the manor, identical in that district with the present boundaries of the City of Manchester, which started in the present Longford Park, the district then known as Melschelache, and proceeded to the region of Upper Chorlton Road along the course of which it then ran. The reference to Chorlton in this context was to Chorlton-on-Medlock. Upper Chorlton Road does indeed form the boundary between the site of the demesne and Old Trafford.

Although this was the earliest known reference to the Hough by name there was a veiled reference to it in a charter of 1248, whereby Henry III granted to Matthew de Hathersage free warren in the demesne lands of his Manor of "Wytinton & Diddesbur" and ordained that none should hunt there or take anything pertaining to free warren therefrom without the consent of Matthew under pain of a fine of ten pounds.

In later times the demesne was known by the names of the Park (15th-17th centuries) and Withington Demesne (18th and 19th centuries). It is, of course, remembered in place names which survive today. Hough End means the boundary of the Hough. It has been suggested that the name means the house at the boundary, the boundary being that between the townships of Withington and Chorlton. This explanation is erroneous. The boundary between these two places was only drawn after 1662. Before that date they were hamlets without fixed boundaries, exactly as Fallowfield is today.

The district in the vicinity of Albemarle Avenue was known in the seventeenth and eighteenth centuries as Park Gate. It was so described in deeds of the period. To this day the large old house in Albemarle Avenue, which is the home of Mr. & Mrs. H. M. Goldberg, is known as Park Cottage. In the nineteenth century a farm in the neighbourhood of Platt Lane Police Station was known as Demesne Farm. Later the district gave its name to Demesne Road.

As regards the villages of the manor the Survey of 1322 mentioned the names of Withington, Didsbury, Barlow, Chorlton, Denton, Haughton Birch, Levenshulme and Le Brokes. To what district the name of Le Brokes applied is, unfortunately, not known. In addition it would seem that Platt, Fallowfield and Rusholme were also in existence by the fourteenth century. There were never villages in either Burnage or Moss Side until modern times.

Turning aside from the larger pictures of the manor to concentrate our attention on that corner of it which is our chief interest, we are immediately faced with the fact that we know almost nothing of the appearance of the actual village of Didsbury in mediaeval times. Before the erection of the artificial banks which now line the river the area below the church must have been a marsh, impenetrable on foot and also impassable by boat. This, no doubt, explains the choice of the site of the church, for it must be borne in mind that while the prime use of the church was always as a place of worship its potential function as a fortress would loom large in the thoughts of its founders. A site with natural defences on two of its four sides could hardly have escaped their notice.

Near the church were natural springs, which would, for obvious reasons, also recommend the place as a defensive position. One of these springs is said to have issued from the roadway in the middle of Stenner Lane and is on record as having been in use in the nineteenth century when it was known as Abercrombie's Well . It was for many hundreds of years the main water supply of the village. Indeed pipes leading from it can still be seen running along the side of a wall and ending at a broken trough near the gate of Fletcher Moss Park. No water comes from it now probably because of the excavations which have taken place in the churchyard. There appears to have been a second spring in the grounds of Stenner Brow.

St. James's Church, of course, stands today on the historic site of the church. The precise date of the foundation of that church is not known. Tradition has fixed it at 1235 but this seems to be based on nothing more than a loose interpretation of a vague observation in Hollingworth's "Mancuniensis", written in the seventeenth century. The first reference to the existence of a church in Didsbury was in the Lancashire Assize Roll of 1246 which mentioned that "William, Chaplain of Dedesbury, came not on the first day; so fined". Fletcher Moss believed that Didsbury had had a church in Saxon times. In view of the fact that the name of Didsbury is itself of Saxon origin it is quite possible that this view was correct.

Apart from the church we have no knowledge whatsoever of the appearance, or indeed of the site, of any individual mediaeval building. The earliest of such information which has come down to us is a seventeenth century description of buildings which stood on the site of Didsbury College of Education.

We can rest assured, however, that the homes of the villagers lay in the immediate vicinity of the church. It seems certain, also, that the open space in front of the Didsbury Hotel was the village green. The title deeds of the Didsbury Hotel show that one Samuel Bethell, the then owner of that property, acquired squatter's rights over this space by enclosing it with boundary stones sometime between 1821 and 1855 and treating it as his own for at least twelve years, during which time nobody came forward with a claim of ownership. The reason that nobody came forward was, of course, that the village green was not in private ownership.

A great deal is known about the location of the open fields in the vicinity of the village. Until surprisingly recently there existed, to the north of Fog Lane, two large fields called Cottonfield and Barcicroft, divided up into strips of the mediaeval pattern. Both these fields are of course remembered in modern street names. The strips lay in bundles arranged at right angles to each other, each bundle being known as a townfield or meanfield. Some of the bundles appear to have had distinctive names, such as the Shutt and the Crabtree Flat. It is tempting to imagine that Cottonfield and Barcicroft were two of the three fields

25

and that the names have descended to us from mediaeval times. Such evidence as is at our disposal, however, suggests that this was not the case. While there seems to be no reason to doubt that the strips themselves were of mediaeval origin the size of Cottonfield and Barcicroft make it appear that they were shrunken remnants of much larger fields. In all probability they were both parts of the same field.

Cottonfield and Barcicroft were, of course, situated equidistant from both Withington and Didsbury. It is not known to which village they appertained. In all probability they were cultivated by men living in both, as well as by such small number of people as lived in cottages in Burnage Lane, known in the Middle Ages as Saltersgate.

Although our knowledge of the other open fields in the district falls far short of what we know of Cottonfield and Barcicroft we are nevertheless able to say with varying degrees of certainty where they lay.

The earliest existing deeds of conveyance of land in Didsbury are dated towards the end of the seventeenth century. One of these was a sale by Thomas Walker and Thomas Walker his son, to Francis Walker of, among other things, the following property:-

"ALL THAT doale or parcel of land lying in a certain mean field called Hoady Botham all which said premises are situate lying and being in Diddesbury aforesaid in the said County of Lancaster."

From the wording of this deed it seems that the meanfield known as Hoady Botham was cultivated in the mediaeval manner as were Cottonfield and Barcicroft. Some confirmation of this is to be found in a late eighteenth century deed which referred to fields known as Hoady Bottoms, Nar Hoady Bottoms, nearest but one Hoady Bottoms, nearest but two Hoady Bottoms and ffarthest Hoady Bottoms. The obvious inference raised by these names is, of course, that they were strips of land arranged one behind the other or, in short, that they were doles. Hoady Botham and Hoady Bottoms can almost certainly be identified with Heathy Bottoms which, it is known, was the mid-nineteenth century name for a field lying between the sites of Didsbury Cricket Ground and Parrs Wood Railway Station.

Even after the disappearance of strip farming a number of fields in the area appear to have retained the name of Townfield. In the eighteenth century Little Townfield lay on what is now Simon Playing Fields, the fields where the South Manchester and District Agricultural Society used to hold its annual show. Clerk's Townfield was near the junction of Didsbury Park and Wilmslow Road. Nearer Townfield and Further Townfield were on the site of Baldock Road, Finney Townfield was in the vicinity of what is now Dene Road. There was also Blomiley's Townfield, the location of which is unknown. On the assumption that these names reveal the existence of strip farming it is clear that the entire central part of Didsbury was so cultivated.

It would also seem that the same system was in operation immediately to the south of Simon's Bridge in the area now occupied by the Didsbury

Golf Club.

At the easterly end of Barcicroft was a district known until modern times as Heaton Wood. This was clearly referred to in the Survey of 1322 as follows:-

> "There is a certain wood there called Hetonwoode of oak trees and suchlike, in which the tenants of Heton who hold in fee by charter have housbote and heybote by the allowance of the lord whereby that wood is much destroyed and not growing up again."

Housbote was the right to cut wood for building purposes. Heybote was the right to cut it for the purpose of building fences.

In all probability the wood stretched at least to the southern end of Burnage Lane, a district known later as Bolton Wood, after which Bolton Avenue derives its name. The name of Parrs Wood suggests that the wood continued on the south side of Didsbury Road also, although the reader should be warned that the historic site of Parrs Wood lies somewhat to the east of the eighteenth century mansion house which bears its name. In the eighteenth century deeds of the house, which was built in 1795, and was for many years the home of the Heald family, the name of Parrs Wood does not appear. If the Tithe Map of Heaton Norris is to be believed, the authentic Parrs Wood was in the vicinity of Heaton Mersey Railway Station.

The Survey of 1322 also recorded that there were, in the wood, 80 acres of common pasture for the tenants of the Manors of Heaton Norris and Withington. Professor Tait pointed out that this was apparently a late example of the villagers of two separate manors sharing the same common, an arrangement which dated back to the period when there was wood and common between the manors but no precise boundary.

There were also another 356 acres of common pasture in Burnage, mentioned in the Survey. The area would be computed in Lancashire acres of 7840 square yards as against 4840 square yards in a statute acre. Such being the case these acres would take up the entirety of Burnage between what we now know as Barcicroft Road and the Cringle Brook, which flows through culverts in the grounds of the Duchess of York Hospital for Babies.

The Survey stated that at some time before 1322 Sir John de Longforde and Sir John Byrom illegally enclosed some 136 acres of the common in defiance of the rights of Sir Thomas Grelle, who was a minor at the time. The date of the occurence was not stated but it is known that Sir John de Longforde was lord of the Manor of Withington between 1284 and 1304, during which years it presumably took place. Sir John Byrom, in addition to being the father of de Longforde's wife Joan, was also the chief tenant of the Grelles in Heaton Norris. The fact that Sir Thomas Grelle, who was, of course, lord of the Manor of Manchester, had land in the area of which he was deprived suggests that Burnage was not at that time considered as being part of the Manor of Withington. It is certainly on record as forming part of that manor in later years.

The common land of the manor was also mentioned in a number of thirteenth century deeds of the de Trafford family which relate to land in and near Rusholme. While we know of the commons in Burnage there is, of course, always the possibility that there were other stretches of common land elsewhere in the manor.

Quite distinct from the common was the moor or waste. The villagers had rights on the common consolidated by the Statute of Merton. The waste was no-man's land between villages or between manors. It was, of course, the property of the lord of the manor. On it the villagers had no rights. Because of the slow development of the area the ancient waste remained moorland until the new techniques introduced by the Agricultural Revolution facilitated its cultivation. As far as the waste adjacent to Didsbury is concerned it lay precisely where one would expect it to lie, between the villages of Didsbury and Withington. The older deeds of land in the vicinity of Parkfield Road, Clyde Road, Old Lansdowne Road, Sandileigh Avenue and Danesmoor Road all referred to it directly. By way of illustration we refer to a deed of 1681 whereby Sir Edward Mosley, the then lord of the manor, conveyed to John Holt a piece of land described as follows:-

"ALL THAT land or parcel of land or new enclosures in Didsbury moor in Withington aforesaid called the Intacke and another inclosure on Didsbury moore in Withington aforesaid called The Five Acres being on the side of the lane leading to a place there called the Red Banke."

The Red Bank was a field where Rowsley Avenue now lies. The lane was, without doubt, the thoroughfare now known as Burton Road. The Intacke and the Five Acres lay along the land where the Midland Hotel, the Barlow Moor Conservative Club and the Albert Park Methodist Church now stand.

It is worthy of note that the names of many of the fields in the area included the words Moor Field. This applies to Clerks Moor Field where Pine Road stands and Lesser Moor Field in the vicinity of Clyde Road and Old Lansdowne Road. The same words occurred, almost without exception, in the names of the fields fronting onto Barlow Moor Road on its south side between Wilmslow Road and the vicinity of Princess Parkway. As they did not occur in field names in any other part of the area there would seem to be reason to believe that the moor extended to the south of Barlow Moor Road. The names Intacke and Rough also appear to have attached only to fields forming part of the moor and since they are common in the vicinity of Darley Avenue, School Lane and Atwood Road, as well as the site of the old West Didsbury Railway Station in Lapwing Lane, we can assume that the moor covered those places also.

Eighteenth century deeds of land in the area make it clear that Didsbury Moor was one and the same place as Barlow Moor, after which an entire district is, of course, named. In addition there exist sixteenth century references to a moor at Chorlton. The Tithe Map of Chorlton prepared, like that of Didsbury, in the middle of the nineteenth century shows fields called Moor Field and Rough in considerable numbers in the present vicinity of Sandy Lane where we may assume that the moor lay.

Little is known of the mediaeval road system of Didsbury but we have already noted a thirteenth century reference to Wilmslow Road in Fallowfield. Although we have no ancient record of that road in Didsbury there can, of course, be no doubt that it continued to the chapel. Burnage Lane can be identified without doubt as the road known as Saltersgate referred to in the Survey of 1322, which mentioned that it was the boundary between Withington and Heaton (Norris). As we have seen the area along the northern stretches of Burnage Lane was common land used by the people of both manors, but south of Green End roundabout the road was indeed the boundary. Between the Renold Works and Didsbury Road it is even today the boundary between Manchester and Stockport. The Survey also mentioned that Saltersgate had been moved from its ancient place. Where its ancient site was we cannot know but it is clear that, in its northerly parts, the course of the road has changed again since the Survey, for it was there recorded that it passed through Reddish.

While Wilmslow Road and Burnage Lane appear to be the only roads out of Didsbury of which ancient records exist, it can safely be assumed that the village was linked by roads to the neighbouring villages of Stockport and Chorlton, from which we may infer that there were roads taking more or less the same course as Didsbury Road and Barlow Moor Road take today. There was also, no doubt, a path leading south from Didsbury to Cheadle along the present course of Wilmslow Road, but there is some reason to believe that this was a very insignificant thoroughfare until the eighteenth century. The road now known as Millgate Lane which continued over the Mersey by means of a ford, and thence led to Gatley, was probably of much greater importance. According to Fletcher Moss it was the main Roman road into Cheshire, but this theory appears to rest on no more reliable evidence than that in the nineteenth century a Roman coin was found nearby.

The position of the road to Northenden must be a matter for some conjecture. In the earliest times all the land in the immediate vicinity of the river would be impassable marshland, but when the land was drained a road would, doubtless, have come into being. Today Stenner Lane leads from the church to the site of the ford which crossed the river where Simon's Bridge now stands. As will be shown in due course, however, the river changed its course during or after the fourteenth century, prior to which it ran considerably to the south of its present course in the neighbourhood of the bridge. In all probability Stenner Lane ran along its present route as far as, say, the large brick barn at the entrance to Fletcher Moss Park, whence it continued in a straight line across the sites of the football fields and Didsbury Golf Course to meet the river, running along its old course, not far from the position of Didsbury Golf Club House. There is no reason to suppose that, in the period which we are discussing the present Ford Lane existed at all.

Of the existence of a corn mill at Didsbury we are quite certain. A deed

29

still exists among the archives of the de Trafford family whereby Sir Simon de Gousil, who at that time was in possession of the manor, released to Henry de Trafford the suit payable by Henry's tenants at Chorlton in respect of Sir Simon's mill at Didsbury. For this Henry was to render to him yearly one pair of gloves and one penny. The mill seems to have stood at the far extremity of Millgate Lane to which it gave its name.

Reference to the water mill leads naturally to the discussion of the part played by the river in Didsbury's history, and to that fascinating subject we must now turn.

Chapter III

THE RIVER

No aspect of Didsbury's history is of more interest than that of the River Mersey. No feature gives rise to more speculation.

The cardinal fact to be borne in mind, the basis on which all deductions must be founded, is that in its natural state the river contained a great deal more water than it does today. The Survey of 1322, when dealing with the water mill at Heaton Norris, stated:-

> "There is a water mill there running by Hertwellesicke worth 16/8d and also a several fishery in Mersee to the midstream of Mersee from Grimesbotham unto Didsbury worth 6d yearly, and this mill from ancient times used to run by Mersee and was then worth 40/- yearly but it is not worth so much for default of water. Nevertheless all the tenants of Heton ought to grind at it to the grain."

What caused the default of water was not explained, but in modern times the construction of the reservoirs in the Peak District, where the sources of the Mersey rise, has further reduced the flow of the water to a fraction of its natural and original volume.

Lying alongside the river in Didsbury and elsewhere, for much of its length, are banks or dykes. That these were constructed by the hand of man is too obvious to require argument. To anyone inspecting the area near the junction of Ford Lane and Stenner Lane it will be clear that before the dykes were erected, and before the water level was reduced below its original state, a great deal of the low lying part of Didsbury must have been a swamp or morass through which the water flowed rather lazily along an ill-defined course. For centuries the lands adjacent to the river were known as eas, ees, or eyes, those words presumably being derived from Anglo-Saxon "ea" or the French "eau", both meaning water. Even on maps of our own day and age the area lying between the river and Dane Road, Sale, is referred to as Sale Ees.

Although it would, at first sight, seem an impossible task to ascertain the date the dykes were erected we find that there is an astonishing abundance of evidence.

W. E. Kay, writing in 1928, mentioned that near the public footpath on Withington Golf Course was the stump of an oak tree which was estimated to be 500 years old. This stump has now, unfortunately, been uprooted and removed. An oak tree, Kay pointed out, will only grow in dry soil. Consequently the land on which it stood must have been dry when it began its long life. For this to have been so the dykes must have been already erected, from which it follows that they date back, at the very latest, to the beginning of the fifteenth century. This argument would seem to be incapable of contradiction.

But there are also other lines of reasoning from which we know that the dykes are considerably older even than Kay suggested.

Turning again to the Survey of 1322 we find the following statement:-

> "Be it known that the lord is disseised . . . . of one rood of land in 2 plots between le Wetheheye and le Warth by William le Smyth of Diddisburie, Robert de Chedle (Cheadle) and dame Matilda de Chole (Chorlton) . . . . the whole of which was taken from waste, except the Warthe."

The Survey made reference, of course, to the entire Manor of Manchester which included, in addition to the Manor of Withington, places as far apart as Blackley, Ashton-under-Lyne and Denton, but the fact that the usurpers came from Didsbury, Cheadle and Chorlton raises the strongest suggestion that the land of which the lord was disseised lay in or near Didsbury. Such being the case it is obvious that the place referred to as "le Warthe" was the same place as the land lying immediately to the south of Simon's Bridge which was referred to in a deed dated in 1597 as the Warthes. The eighteenth century field names in that area included, in almost every case, the word "Warth". The location of le Wethehey is nothing like as certain, but it is known that in the eighteenth and nineteenth centuries, and indeed in the early part of the twentieth century as well, the Simon Playing Fields were known as the Withy Ley. It was probably the same place that was referred to as Whitley in a court case fought in 1600. It does not require great imagination to accept at least the possibility that the names Withy Ley and Whitley were derived from Wetheheye. If such was the case the land of which the lord of the Manor of Manchester was disseised would, of course, have been the land now occupied by Stenner Lane Football Fields.

Now it would appear to be obvious that William le Smyth and his associates would hardly have been likely to disseise the lord of a worthless swamp. And for what possible reasons would part of a swamp be dignified with names such as Le Wetheheye and Le Warthe, which latter name means a meadow on the side of the water? All the evidence in the Survey most surely indicates that by 1322 the swamp had become dry land, which is another way of saying that the dykes were in existence.

But we can take the argument even further. It has already been pointed out that Simon de Gousil had a mill at the end of Millgate Lane. Clearly this would not have been erected before the dykes or it too would have stood in the swamp. Quite apart from the obvious inconvenience of such a thing it would have added enormously to the work involved in erecting the mill to choose such a place to rest its foundations. Furthermore before the dykes were erected the river would have flowed far too sluggishly across the flat lands to turn a mill wheel with the required force. Consequently it would seem probable, to say the least, that the dykes were built during Simon's lifetime or even, perhaps, before his birth.

Simon de Gousil's deed of release of Henry de Trafford is not dated but it is known that in 1278 he was involved in litigation at Lancaster Assizes so that we can date the deed as belonging roughly to the latter part of the thirteenth century. The details of one of the cases in which he was involved form fascinating reading in connection with the subjects at present being discussed:-

"The Assize came to enquire if John de Birum, Simon de Gousle, Robert fil Sewall, Robert fil Stephen, Richard fiz la Vidue and Robert fil Sampson had recently unlawfully erected a certain dyke in Didsbury to the hurt of the free tenant, William de Didsbury, and why he complains that they have raised the said dyke to the like hurt of him, the free tenant, so that whereas he was accustomed to have a right of way with his horses and his oxen, calves, yearlings and other animals direct from his house to his common pasture in Didsbury he is now obliged to go round nearby one league with his animals. And John came and answers on behalf of himself and all the others and says that he has done no injury or ejection, nor has he erected any dyke to the hurt of the aforesaid free tenant, William, in that town. Thus he declares. Because he says that the aforesaid William has sufficient egress and right of way to his pasture with all his animals, and also regress, and he says that the aforesaid dyke about which the aforesaid William is complaining has been erected, in no way to the hurt of the said William, half a league from his house. Thus he declares and concerning this matter he places himself on the Assize.

The jury say upon their oath that the aforesaid John and the others have laid a claim to a quarter of the aforesaid dyke, nearly ten perches long, to the hurt of the free tenant, William, in Didsbury, just as he alleges. And the Order of the Court is that the aforesaid quarter of the aforesaid dyke should be demolished at the expense of the aforesaid John and the others. And he, William, should have his right of way with his animals. And the aforesaid John and the others are condemned. And similarly the aforesaid William is condemned in respect of his false claim concerning three perches of the aforesaid dyke, erected otherwise than to his hurt, etc."

With the equipment and techniques available in the Middle Ages the erection of the dykes must have been a prodigious operation. It is not too much to say that it would have kept every able bodied man in the Manor

33

of Withington occupied for months, if not years. The question we must now ask ourselves is why the then lord of the manor, whether it was Simon de Gousil, or a predecessor or a successor, should have undertaken such an enormous task. The explanation which springs most rapidly to mind is that the purpose of the undertaking was to reclaim land for agriculture but this can be dismissed out of hand. It is known that as late as the second half of the eighteenth century there was ample uncultivated land to the north of the village on Didsbury Moor. Had the village been hungry for land this would surely have been brought into cultivation.

The only other possible explanation lies in the suggestion already made that before the operation the course of the river was ill-defined and its flow sluggish. In order to get it into the fast flowing and controlled state necessary to work a mill it would first be necessary to erect the dykes. The alternative to the immense expenditure of labour involved would presumably have been starvation for lack of bread.

At some time the course of the River Mersey in the stretches that flow past Didsbury and Chorlton has changed. A glance at the map will show that while it is broadly true to say that the southern boundary of Didsbury, and therefore of the Manor of Withington, was the present course of the Mersey there were four parts of Didsbury and two parts of Chorlton on the south side of the river while there were three parts of Northenden on the north side. It does not require to be pointed out that the probable cause of these "islands" was the change in the river's position.

There exists to this day, at the bottom of Longley Lane, Northenden, a dell with stagnant water at the bottom of which grow a number of willow trees. The level of the ground drops sharply to the water. This was part of the old river bed. An observer who does not object to getting his shoes caked with mud and his trousers fouled by long vegetation, can follow the old course of the river in a northerly direction for quite some distance.

There is very little evidence indeed as to the date or even the century that the river changed its course at any point. The Survey of 1322 described the boundary of the Manor of Manchester, which at its southern end was also the boundary of the Manor of Withington, as "following the Mere-broke as far as the confluence of Tame and Mersey and then following the Mersey into the Stretford-broke and Chollerton". The Tame and the Mersey meet in the centre of Stockport, the Stret-forde-broke is generally identified with Chorlton Brook which flows into the Mersey near Stretford. Since the areas on the south of the present river bed were undoubtedly part of the Manor of Manchester the Survey suggests, on the face of it, that it was prepared before the river changed its course. It can, of course, be suggested, possibly with justification, that the author of the Survey was using a broad generalisation and did not consider small deviations important enough to mention. It would appear however that he was not dealing in broad generalisations. When describing the boundaries or other parts of the manor he went into great detail. The boundary he recorded, ran "between Brere-rydinge and the Maisterfeld, by a hedge as far as the midstream of Irke" and later "to a field, garden or orchard of ancient inclosure as far as the Redebroke". It is hardly likely—and one cannot put it in stronger terms—that a surveyor defining the boundary by reference to a hedge and a garden would overlook areas as large as the bend in the river going round Didsbury Golf Course. Consequently it would seem that in 1322 the boundary of the manor was indeed the river, or in other words, that the river had not then altered its course.

Further evidence of the date of the change is contained in a memorandum endorsed on the deed whereby the manor was conveyed to Rowland Mosley in 1597. In feudal times it was a matter of great importance for a land transfer to be a matter of public knowledge since every lord wished to know who the tenants were from whom he was entitled to services and every tenant needed to know to which lord the services were owed. Consequently it was the practice, on the sale of real estate, for the vendor and the purchaser to meet on or near the site when the vendor would actually hand over a twig or sod of earth to the purchaser and say "Enter on this land and God give you joy." or something to the same effect. This would be done in the presence of witnesses. If it was not convenient for the parties to attend the ceremony personally they could appoint agents.

On the back of the deed of 1597 are a number of memoranda recording the performance of just such ceremonies of which the following is one:-

"Memorandum that ye xxixth daye of Marche in the yeare wthin wrytten possession and seisin was taken and delyved by Charles Leighe one of the atturneys wthin mtend to the wthin named Nicholas Mosley atturney to ye wthin named Rowlande Mosley to ye saide Rowlande Mosley his use & of his heires & assignes for on of and in one piece of lande called Watersyd lyeinge and beinge in ye hammel of Didisburye & towneshippe of Withington in name of all & singular ye landes &hereditamts beyonde ye water called Gatley eye accordinge to ye tenor of ye same deed."

This memorandum was signed by no less than ten witnesses which means that in all probability the majority of the educated people of the manor was present.

Gatley Eye was the land now on the south side of the Mersey adjacent to Gatley Brook. It is at present occupied in part by a Manchester Corporation refuse tip and in part by Didsbury Golf Course. The memorandum does, of course, prove that at that stretch, at least, the course of the river changed before 1597.

It would seem then that the river shifted its course after 1322 and before 1597. Unfortunately we cannot come to a more accurate conclusion from the information at our disposal.

From this reasoning something further arises. If the dykes were erected before 1322, and the course of the river did not alter until after that year, it follows that the course must have been changed artificially. Both Kay and Fletcher Moss accepted without question or explanation that this was in fact the case; but for what reason the lords of the Manors of

35

Withington, Northenden and Cheadle joined forces to execute this second prodigious operation is a mystery. Could it have been that in some way the wide bends regulated the flow of the water to a speed suitable to the water mills?

There are numerous features of historical interest along the river as it flows through Didsbury.

It enters the area of the township near Cheadle Bridge, the crossing being known in the early part of the seventeenth century as the Boat, changing to Cheadle Boat towards the end of that century. At the end of the eighteenth century the farmhouse standing on the Didsbury bank was known as Boathouse Farm. These names imply, of course, that there was a ferryboat on the site. Yet all the contemporary accounts of the passage of Bonnie Prince Charlie's army across the river in 1745 refer to the spot as Cheadle Ford. Was the crossing a ferry or a ford? The question is, perhaps, made simpler by an entry in the accounts of the Manchester to Wilmslow Turnpike Trust:-

8th August, 1759.   Paid Mr. Broome for the loss of his
                     Ferry at Cheadle Ford and one year's   84 : 0 : 0
                     interest".

The depth of the water under Cheadle Bridge is, at present, between two and three feet in fair weather. In the eighteenth century the water would have been a little deeper. Probably wheeled traffic used the place as a ford while at the same time there was a ferry boat available for pedestrians.

The crossing found a place in history when the Jacobite army crossed the river there on 1st December, 1745. The details of that event will be related in their proper place. All that need be said here is that they are on record, erroneously, as having built a bridge. Fletcher Moss's version of the occurrence concluded that their bridge stood until it collapsed in 1756.

Quite apart from the unlikelihood that a bridge erected in a matter of hours, by men lacking either the proper equipment or the technical knowledge, would have stood for eleven years and carried for part of that period the traffic of a major road, there is clear proof that it was not so. Fletcher Moss failed to observe an advertisement in the Manchester Mercury of 4th November, 1755, which read as follows:-

NOTICE IS HEREBY GIVEN
That any person willing to undertake the building of a Cart Bridge over the River Mersey at Cheadle Ford, betwixt Cheshire and Lancashire, which was undertaken to have been built by James Marshall late of Nether Knutsford, in the County of Chester, Mason, deceased may apply immediately to John Swinton and Peter Swinton of Nether Knutsford aforesaid, Tanners, Representatives of the said James Marshall who will be ready to treat and agree with any proper Person for the building of the said Bridge and also for the Materials provided for that purpose by the said James Marshall in his lifetime."

36

It will be observed that James Marshall was a mason from which we may infer that his bridge was made of stone.

The bridge was completed by a contractor called Henshaw. He must have been incompetent at his work for we find the following entry in the parish register on 8th July, 1756, only eight months after the publication of the advertisement:-

"John, Son of Thos. Smith of Didsbury killed by the fall of ye bridge".

Thomas Smith was at that time the tenant of the farmhouse. The Manchester Mercury, reporting the event on 13th July, 1756, observed that another person also was wounded so that his life was despaired of.

A second bridge was built by John Knight and his partners in 1758 but this stood for little more than 20 years. The third permanent bridge was built in 1780. It was demolished in 1861 to make way for the present one.

Before we leave the subject of Cheadle Boat, we should point out that in the late seventeenth and early eighteenth centuries it was the practice of the church wardens of Didsbury to make an annual visit to the place, but their purpose in doing so is not known.

Flowing past the present site of the Galleon Swimming Pool the river came to a small island which lay just to the east of the present site of Kingsway. A water mill was erected here in 1810. It was built spanning the arm of the river which divided the island from the mainland, that being utilised as the mill race. A weir was erected a few yards past the mouth of the race. From the Cheshire side of the river the opening of the mill race can still be seen as can the battered remains of the weir. The mill race was filled in at some time in the nineteenth century and the mill building demolished a few years ago.

A little further downstream on the present sites of Parklands Drive and Jayton Avenue, there were fields known in the eighteenth century as Nar Boat Field and ffurther Boat Fields. These names seem to suggest that at some period a ferry boat operated here as well but if such was the case nothing is known of its history.

About a quarter of a mile still further downstream were fields known in the eighteenth century as Midup and Mill Hey. The names Midup, Middup or Mydoppe, while their exact connotation is uncertain, were connected in some way with the presence of a mill. That a mill stood in the vicinity is beyond question. It is to that mill that Millgate Lane, formerly known as Millgate, Milnegate or Mylnegate, owes its name. Although we cannot be certain about the matter it is probable that the original mill of Simon de Gousil stood on this spot. No visible trace of any kind now remains of it.

It might here be pertinent to give a full account of Simon de Gousil's release of Henry de Trafford. Written in Latin on parchment measuring not more than 7¼" by 3½" it ran:-

"To all the faithful of Christ to whom the present writing shall come Symon de Gousil, Knight, Greeting in the Lord. Know ye that I have remised and entirely quit claimed on behalf of myself and my heirs and assigns to Henry de Trafford and his heirs or assigns the homage of the said Henry and his heirs and each and every rent that the said Henry has been obliged and accustomed to pay to me annually for all his lands and holdings which he holds of me in divers places in the fee of Withington. Moreover I have remised and entirely quit claimed to the said Henry and his heirs or assigns every kind of suit of my mill at Didsbury concerning all his men of Chorlton and the duty to improve, repair and make the pool of the aforesaid mill and every kind of service, exaction, custom and demand, specified and unspecified, in which the said Henry or his heirs or his men are obliged to me and my heirs by reason of the aforesaid holdings; he rendering homage to the chief lord of Manchester and rendering to him annually at the Feast of St. Michael one pair of gloves and one penny for all secular service exaction custom and demand. That is to say that for ever hereinafter neither I nor my heirs, nor anyone through me or in my name, shall be able to enforce or lay claim to obtain any right or claim in the aforesaid homage, rents, suits or duty to improve, repair or make the aforesaid pool or in any other services as aforesaid. In witness whereof I have affixed my seal to this present writing; these being witnesses, Sir Geoffrey de Bracebridge, Knight, Geoffrey de Chadderton, Richard de Radcliff, Richard de Moston, Robert de Prestwich, Jordan de Crompton and many others".

The original of this document is among the de Trafford muniments at the Lancashire County Record Office, Preston.

A little further downstream still the river enters into the first of the great bends which are such a notable characteristic of its course through Didsbury. The bend so formed, now comprising the Didsbury Refuse Tip, was know as the Great Eye. At the apex of the bend, that is to say at the extremity of Millgate Lane, was Gatley Ford which, as we shall see, was used as a crossing place by a mounted patrol of Prince Charles's army on the day before the main crossing. The field on the Lancashire side of the ford was known as Gatley Ford Meadow, Sandfield or Gatley Warth although it was also referred to as the Soonts.

The river flows on round Didsbury Golf Course, which stands on land which, as we have seen, was known as the Warths or Northen Eyes. On the northern extremity of this land was Northenden Ford. Nothing is known of the origins of this ancient crossing place. The earliest known reference to it was contained in a letter written on 21st May, 1645, by Sir William Brereton, a Parliamentary commander in the Civil War. To this letter we shall have ample cause to refer again. Referring to the crossing places along the river he listed:-

" . . . . Haleford, Ronchorne Foard below Warrington and Thelwall foard, Erlamfoard, Crosfoard Bridge, Ashton Bridge, Carington Bridg, Northerden Boate and foard, Stockport Bridg . . . . and divers other undefensible passes where-with I am well acquainted."

The interesting feature of this quotation is not what it includes but what it omits. It makes no reference to Cheadle Ford. Brereton, it is known, lived in Handforth, to which the main road from Manchester went over Cheadle Bridge right up to the opening of the Kingsway Extension in recent years. Consequently one would have thought that he would have crossed Cheadle Ford many times. The absence of any reference to it suggests that at the time it was so insignificant a place as not to merit mention except, perhaps, as one of the "divers other indefensible passes". Clearly Brereton thought it of less importance than Northenden Ford. After the erection of the bridge it became of great importance and by the end of the eighteenth century the road over it was part of the coach road from Manchester to London.

The iron bridge over the river which replaced the ford was built in 1901 with funds provided by Henry Simon, father of the late Lord Simon of Wythenshawe, to give easy access to the Poor's Field which lay on the site of the present car park of Didsbury Golf Club. A full account of it was given by Fletcher Moss in "Fifty Years Public Work in Didsbury".

Northenden Boat was the site of a ferry boat which crossed the river where the Tatton Arms now stands. At this point the water is seven feet deep in good weather, due to the weir which still stands a few yards downstream. As the spot is in the immediate vicinity of Northenden village some means of crossing the water was clearly required.

On the 16th March, 1539, Sir Ralph Longford, lord of the Manor of Withington, sold a piece of land to Robert Tatton of Wythenshawe. In consideration of £6.13.4d. he declared:-

"I have given, committed, and by this present writing confirmed to the said Robert all my land in Didsbury in the County of Lancaster lying along the water of Mersey which flows between Northenden in the County of Chester and Didsbury in the said County of Lancaster called the Myddoppe being near the land of the said Robert Tatton called the Mylle Hille and Kenworthee Ee in the said County of Chester and which said parcel of land extends also to the weir and mill of the said Robert forty roods in length along the water of Mersey and also a certain waterfall or weir made situated and strengthened in the water of the aforesaid Mersey to keep and confirm the flow of that water to a certain mill of the said Robert built above the water and also free passage going and returning with one boat for the said Robert in, through and over the said water and the right to dig fix and set piles post stakes poles and other instruments necessary in and on all the land of me the said Ralph in Didsbury aforesaid."

The mill referred to was the mill in Mill Lane Northenden, the successor of which was demolished in 1966 to make way for a car park. The Myddoppe was the island which lay on the south side of the river, adjacent to Palatine Road, until the filling in of the narrow arm of the river, formerly used as the mill race, joined it to Northenden. It is now the site of a petrol station. Mill Hill was the field just south of the river

39

through the site of which Palatine Road runs. Kenworthy Ee was the old name for land now occupied by Northenden Golf Course.

In modern times the island is considered as being in Northenden and was shown as being in that place on the map of Northenden, prepared in 1641, which now hangs in Wythenshawe Hall. Yet it was described in the deed as being in Didsbury. This was clearly a very late example of a political boundary being determined according to the legal ownership of the lands it divided. When the island belonged to the lord of the Manor of Withington it was in Didsbury and Lancashire. Once it had been sold to Robert Tatton it became part of Northenden and Cheshire.

A few days after this conveyance we find Longford and Tatton entering into another agreement. After reciting that Robert Tatton and his ancestors had "from time whereof man's mind is not to the contrary" made attachment of their weir on Longford's land in Didsbury it went on to confirm Tatton's right to fix attachments of the weir on Longford's land and further granted to Tatton "power and authority to have manage and sail a boat in and upon the said Water of Mersey between the land of the said Ralph in Didsbury aforesaid and the land of the said Robert Tatton in Northenden aforesaid to carry and recarry folks horses and baggage and to tie and fix to the land the said boat upon the land of the said Ralph in Didsbury aforesaid to posts stakes and any other things apt or convenient for the same as best shall like and please the said Robert Tatton his heirs and assigns and also free passage and repassage for the said Robert and his heirs and all other folks coming and repairing to the said Water of Mersey through and over the land of the said Ralph Longford in Didsbury aforesaid".

The right of way referred to at the end of this passage still exists in the form of a pathway which leads from the vicinity of the Tatton Arms, past the Club House of Withington Golf Club, to the northern end of Simon's Bridge. The land over which this path leads was known as Didsbury Eea.

Thus, as far as we can see, began the ferry which is now remembered in the name as Boat Lane, Northenden. The crossing became known as Northenden Boat and was one of the places referred to by Sir William Brereton in the letter to which we have just referred.

During the Civil War the Tattons were found to be paying the lords of the Manor of Withington a rent of 4/- per annum for the privilege of fixing their weir on Didsbury Eea. These payments were made until at least the end of the eighteenth century.

Passing under Northenden Bridge the river flows in a northerly direction with Northenden Golf Course on its west bank. On its east bank lies land which for centuries was known as Lum Farm, the farmhouse being at what is now the junction of Mersey Road and Spath Road. In the vicinity of the farm there was yet another ford all trace of which has been lost. It was shown on certain estate maps of the Tatton family produced in 1830 but by 1845 it had disappeared. The path leading to it on the Didsbury side of the river was near the present position of the Beeches.

The river flows round a sharp loop at the northerly end of Northenden

Golf Course and here it leaves Didsbury to flow between Chorlton and Northenden.

At this point we leave the Mersey to its never ending progress to the sea. Many English rivers are more beautiful; few, except the Thames, are so steeped in history.

Chapter IV

DIDSBURY IN THE CIVIL WARS

The part played by Didsbury in the Civil Wars has hitherto been overlooked by history. As far as can be seen no history of Manchester treats of the subject, and certainly it is scarcely mentioned in any of the histories of Didsbury. Yet it is not too much to say that an event occurred in the district which changed the whole course of the war. It may even have changed the course of British history.

It is said that the first shots of the war were fired in Manchester on 15th July, 1642, when Lord Strange, son of the Earl of Derby, and leader of the Royalist elements in Lancashire and Cheshire, marched on the town and demanded ten barrels of gunpowder which were refused by the Parliamentarians. After the failure of negotiations a skirmish ensued, after which Lord Strange withdrew into Cheshire. The route of his withdrawal is not known but it may well have been through Withington and Didsbury. Certainly his forces must have passed nearby.

Didsbury may thus have had its first taste of the war at a very early stage, although no trace of such an experience has survived in records. For that we must pass to the siege of Manchester, which began on 25th September, 1642, when Lord Strange returned with 4,000 foot soldiers, 200 dragoons, 100 light cavalry and seven pieces of cannon. His ultimatum to the townspeople was rejected by them and his artillery answered with musketry fire. Lord Strange set up his headquarters during the siege at Alport Lodge in the vicinity of Knott Mill. This was the property of Sir Edward Mosley of Hough End and was apparently destroyed during the fighting. On 1st October he gave up the struggle, fearful perhaps that his army, which he had recruited from his Lancashire tenantry, could not be relied upon to fight against the townspeople of Manchester, with whom they had so much in common.

A contemporary account of the siege described the casualties:-

42

"There were slain on Lord Strange's side (as we credibly heard) about two hundred, and some commanders of note, three whereof were buried at Didsbury; and the town lost but four men, whereof two by accident and two by the enemy, but no more in all."

The parish register of Didsbury contains the following entry made in 1642:-

"Mr. Thomas Hebelthwaites was buried at Didsburie the xxviijth of Septembr this gentleman came Anno Dni 1642 against Manchestr and was slaine at the siege there and was brought to Didsburie to bee buryed and was buryed by Mr. Turner Schoolmaister."

No mention was made in the register of the other two members of the Royalist army who were said to have been buried in the churchyard. This omission is probably explained by an entry which was made more or less immediately after Mr. Hebelthwaites' funeral:-

"At this tyme was sivill and bloodie warrs betwixt King Charles and his Parlament and Manchester was besieged the 25 of this month and this book was plundered by T:W: wch caused this blanke."

There were no further entries in the book until the burial of Margerie Norres took place on 13th February, 1644. The letters T.W. must have represented the initials of Thomas Wood, the parish clerk. He died in October, 1651, having held the office of clerk for about sixty years. The word plundered in the context meant hidden.

The reason why Thomas Wood thought it advisable to hide the register was, doubtless, because of the presence of the Parliamentary troops in Manchester. The Parliamentary forces showed scant respect for the churches as the story of many a parish church shows. He probably hid not only the Register but the rest of the church's records and valuables as well. While the register was eventually restored and used again, it may be that the other contents of the parish chest were never replaced. Very few records dated prior to the war can now be traced although several documents survived from the 1650's.

While it is clear enough why the register was hidden the timing of its restoration offers something of a puzzle. It took place during the time of the siege of Wythenshawe Hall, when a Parliamentary force under Colonel Dukinfield besieged the hall, which was defended for the Royalists by its owner, Robert Tatton. The siege began in November, 1642, and lasted until 25th February, 1644, when the arrival of two cannon from Manchester settled the issue. At that time Parliamentary soldiers must have been a regular sight in the district. Why was the book, which had remained carefully concealed from them for eighteen months, brought out of hiding to record the funeral of Margerie Norres only twelve days before the struggle at Wythenshawe Hall reached its climax? Here is a mystery indeed.

Almost immediately after the funeral of Margerie Norres the following entry was made in the list of burials in the register:-

<blockquote>"Ric' Ward gent: a troop   Ffebruarie 16"</blockquote>

Richard Ward was, doubtless, one of the Parliamentary force fighting at Wythenshawe. In all one officer and three soldiers were killed on the Parliamentary side. If any besides Richard Ward were buried at Didsbury the funerals must have taken place whilst the register was still hidden.

Of the Royalist force who defended the hall the following record remains:-

<blockquote>"The persons hereunder named went into, were in or were sent to the Garrison at Wythenshawe against the Parliament, viz, Thomas Mallory, clerke: Robert Twyford and Richard his brother; Henry Pendleton of Manchester; Edward Carter, clerke and William Carter, the late organist at Manchester; Edward Legh of Baguley Esq; Mr. Richard Vawdrey; Mr. John Bretland and his man. And theise inhabitants of Northenden: James Renshall, Henry and Robert his sonnes, Humphrey Savage, Thomas Hampson, Henry Coppocke, James Deane, Edmund Prestwych, and his two sons Edmund and John, Roger Rowson of Kenerden, Raphe and James Brownehill of the Moorside, John Poween of the Moorside. Out of Baguley, Wm. Hamnett, Robert Chapman and Nicholas his Brother, Thomas Hill. Out of Gatley, Raphe Savage, Robert Torkington and John Blomiley. Out of Etchells, William Bailey and his sonne. Out of Didsbury, Harry Tipping, Alexander Coppocke, William Piggott. One William Clarke and John Blomiley were in the Garrison.

And also that Robert Deane of Altrincham, Hugh Newton, Richard Grantham of Hale, Robert his sonne, George Delahey of Timperley Andrew Winterbotham alias Pole, and his brother Raphe, Lawrence Hardy, Thomas Barlow, John Cockson of Sharson greene in Northenden, William Hopwood, Richard Smith, Harry Banister, Lawrence Walker of Didsbury and Thomas Lynney of the same, were in the Garrison."</blockquote>

It will be observed that Robert Tatton himself was not mentioned in the list. He managed to escape from Wythenshawe and made his way to Chester, where he took part in the defence of that town when it was besieged.

Richard Twyford was the brother-in-law of Robert Tatton, having married his sister Margaret. His elder brother Robert Twyford, who it will be noticed was also in the garrison, was the great grandfather of Rev. Robert Twyford, and the great, great grandfather of Rev. William Twyford who, in succession, were ministers of Didsbury Chapel from 1726 to 1795. Before the war he had been steward of the Manchester Court Leet.

After the war Richard and Robert, both of them Didsbury men, were punished with thousands of others for their allegiance to the King by the forfeiture of their estates. They were, however, allowed to redeem the estates on payment of fines, assessed by the Committee of Sequestrations. Richard Twyford was fined £44; his brother Robert was fined £45.15.4d.

Lawrence Walker was almost certainly the person of that name whose baptism was recorded in the Didsbury parish register on 12th January, 1599. He died in September, 1671, and was the owner of a house and farm on the present site of Didsbury College of Education.

Little or nothing is known of the other Didsbury men taken at Wythenshawe but the parish register mentioned a few persons of the same names at dates which show it to be possible that they took part in the siege. In the case of Thomas Linney, who died in 1673, we are told that he lived at Lane End. This is thought to have been the district on the north bank of the Mersey where Simon's Bridge now stands.

No sooner had the victor of Wythenshawe, Colonel Dukinfield, seen his efforts crowned with success than another task awaited him. The King's nephew, Prince Rupert, was advancing from Cheshire to the relief of Lathom House, near Ormskirk, besieged by the Parliamentarians, and tenaciously defended by the Countess of Derby.

> "on ffryday the xxiijth of Maye 1644 the Prince with his army advanced towards Lancashire & did quarter in and about Knottesford. And on Saturdaye they advanced to Stockporte where Colonell Duckinfield and Colonell Maynwaringe laye with theire forces of horse and foote, beinge not able to wthstand soe potent an Enymy. And The Townesmen Alsoe wth all theire horse & foote upon the advance of them fled into Lancashire. And on Sondaye ytt was reported that the Prince had entered into Lancashire and weire at Barloe More, and had somoned Manchester. The next week followinge . . . . Prince Rupert with his Army beinge in Lancashire, marched from Barloe More over the fforde neere Eccles and within twoe or three dayes after assaulted Boulton; And wth losse of many on bothe sides, wonne ytt, and used much Creweltie by inhuman murthers in the Towne."

Barloe More was, of course, Barlow Moor, also known as Didsbury Moor. We cannot be certain what the extent of this piece of waste land was in 1644, but it certainly included the land now occupied by Parkfield Road, Old Lansdowne Road, Clyde Road, Danesmoor Road and Sandileigh Avenue. It may also have stretched far enough to take in the sites of Atwood Road and Beaver Road, the land immediately south of Barlow Moor Road and the land in the vicinity of Nell Lane and Southern Cemetery. The Prince's army would, no doubt, have bivouacked on that part of it nearest to the village, that is to say somewhere near where Emmanuel Church and Didsbury Library stand now.

Prince Rupert and his officers would have taken up quarters in the village itself. But where in the Didsbury of that time was there a house fit for a Prince? As we have seen the Walker family owned a house where the Didsbury College of Education now stands. They were people of wealth and their house was probably the best appointed in the village. Perhaps the Prince slept under their roof. There is some fragmentary evidence which suggests the possibility that the Cock Inn was in existence at that time. Probably, also, there was an inn on the site of the Didsbury Hotel, kept by Thomas Wood; not the parish clerk but a relative of his. However many inns there were in the vicinity we may rest assured that Rupert's troops patronised them.

Having defeated Colonels Dukinfield and Mainwaring at Stockport, Rupert does not appear to have encountered serious opposition until he arrived at Bolton. That the Parliamentary sympathies of the Manchester townspeople were not shared by their neighbours in the surrounding hamlets is demonstrated in another contemporary account which mentioned that by 5th June, after they had taken Bolton, the Royalist army, which was 8,000 strong at Stockport, was double that number. For this astounding growth the account blamed the help given to the Prince by the Earl of Derby (the former Lord Strange, who had by then succeeded to the family title) and "the Popish gentry of Lancashire", but it must be remembered that the earl could only work with the material he had at hand. All the evidence suggests that, in the main, the country people living to the south and west of Manchester were strongly Royalist in their sympathies, in marked contrast, it may here be observed, to their neighbour Charles Worsley of Platt Hall who, at the time of Prince Rupert's sojourn at Barlow Moor, was a captain in the Parliamentary army.

It can surely be taken for granted that during his stay at Barlow Moor the Prince recruited men from Didsbury and Withington into his force but as to their number, their identities and their fortunes the records are silent.

The route by which Rupert's army reached Barlow Moor from Stockport must have been by Didsbury Road, Parrs Wood Lane and Wilmslow Road. When they left for Eccles they would have moved up Barlow Moor Road. After sacking Bolton they advanced to Liverpool which they took by storm and then to Lathom House. From there they were ordered by the King to cross the Pennines and relieve the siege of York, but the Parliamentary armies lying before that city proved too strong for them and they were disastrously defeated on 2nd July, 1644, at Marston Moor.

The victory at Marston Moor gave rise to a controversy in the Parliamentary camp. Some of its leaders believed that the King would be willing to accept terms. Cromwell, on the other hand, took the view that he must be harried to the end. After bitter quarrels his view prevailed, with the result that the Parliamentary forces were re-organised into a "New Model Army", which, in the spring of 1645, set out to attack the King at Oxford, where his headquarters had been located for almost the whole of the war. Despite a minor victory at Lostwithiel in Cornwall, Charles had now realised that the end was near and determined to march north.

His main reason for doing so was to relieve Chester, besieged by the Parliamentary army under Sir William Brereton, which was, at that time, a seaport and the gateway to Ireland, from whence he had already received reinforcements and hoped to receive more. It seems that a second reason was that he was aiming to reach Scotland to join up with the Earl of Montrose who had raised a force of Scottish Royalists and won a series of quite remarkable victories.

The Parliamentary leaders seem to have been more determined to prevent Charles reaching Scotland than to preserve the siege of Chester. In particular they viewed with alarm the prospect of his marching through Lancashire, where he might have been able to reinforce his army, as Prince Rupert had done the previous year. It was therefore decided to hold him on the Mersey at all costs, but the main Parliamentary forces of the north under the command of Lord Fairfax, were in Yorkshire, and apart from a relatively small number of troops in Cheshire, most of them engaged in the siege of Chester, the approaches to Lancashire were undefended.

In order to reach Scotland Charles would almost certainly have had to pass through either Stretford or Stockport. To advance west of Stretford would have been difficult for in that direction lay Chat Moss, which in those days was a bog, across which the passage of heavy transport was out of the question. To the east of Stockport rose the Pennines, almost as great an obstacle. It was then to the stretch of the River Mersey between Stretford and Stockport that all eyes were turned, although the Parliamentarians took good care to see that the route through Warrington, which lay to the west of Chat Moss, was also guarded.

The Parliamentary leaders were, of course, in a dilemma. If they mustered at Stretford the King would try to cross at Stockport, and vice-versa. Sir William Brereton realised that a number of alternative routes were open to his adversary. Reporting to his superiors, in London, on 21st May he gloomily observed:-

> "I doe believe it to be most impossible to keep the passes into Lancashire which I know to be very many and in the judgement of all those soldiers with whome I have conferred it is conceived of most dangerous consequence, seeing there are many of them; as Haleford, Ronchorne Foard below Warrington and Thelwall Foard, Erlam Foard, Crosfoard Bridg, Ashton Bridg, Carington Bridg, Northerden Boate and foard, Stockport Bridg, where Prince Rupert passed the last yeare and divers other indefensible passes wherewith I am well aquainted, besides I have heard of divers other foards and passes."

This assessment painted a rather blacker picture than was justified. As we have seen Chat Moss formed a natural barrier on which the Parliamentarians could rely. Even if the King had crossed at Irlam Ford, Carrington Bridge or Ashton Bridge he would still have had to march east, on the north bank of the river, until he reached Stretford.

In the light of all his difficulties Brereton took the obvious course. He decided to deploy his forces in a position on the north bank of the Mersey, equidistant from both Stretford and Stockport, so as to be able to meet an attack coming from either direction. That position was, of course, Didsbury. The decision was not tactical, it was strategic. As soon as the Parliamentarians formed the view that Charles was heading for Scotland there could have been no other choice. Where else was there a major river to the west of the Pennines which could only be crossed on a front of seven miles?

An advance east of the Pennines would not have caused the King any fewer problems. As we have seen considerable Parliamentary forces lay at York.

Messages were therefore sent out to Parliamentary forces in all parts of the north of England ordering them to assemble, on 22nd May, 1645, on Barlow Moor, the same spot where Prince Rupert's troops had camped almost exactly twelve months earlier. Much of the correspondence which passed between the Parliamentary commanders during this period has survived. On 19th May, Brereton, then at his headquarters in Nantwich, sent an order to Colonel Ashton, one of his subordinates before Chester:-

> "It is this day ordered that Coll: Ashton wth his Rgt of ffoote now in Cheshire march into Lancash: and that ye sd Coll Ashton doe bring ye sd Regt as Compleate as possible to ye Randezvous at Barlymore in Lancash: upon Thursday and there Remaine in a body until further Order according to ye Comand received from ye Committee of both kingdomes and ye Lord Farefax.
>
> Wm Brereton."

In the event the muster on Barlow Moor was a failure. Brereton himself made the mistake of believing that no front was as important as the one on which his own army was engaged. He reluctantly and belatedly abandoned the siege of Chester, but he left some of his army in the outlying positions so as to contain the defenders, at least in some degree, and to prevent Charles from entering the city. In fact he marched to Barlow Moor with his face turned in the direction of Chester. Many of the Parliamentary troops in Lancashire flatly refused to go there on the grounds that it was too near to Manchester, which just at that time was in the grip of the plague, a fact noted in the Didsbury parish register. Others refused to go because their pay was in arrear. The commanders of the Parliamentary forces which were besieging Lathom House, near Ormskirk, suffered from the same failing as Brereton. They refused to lift the siege even to prevent the passage of the King himself.

The greatest disappointment was the Covenanters' Army, an army of Scots, allied to Parliament, which lay at Ripon. Writing to Brereton on 21st May, its commander, Lord Leven, announced his intention of marching to Westmorland so as to form a second line of defence. He accordingly marched across the Pennines. At the height of the crisis his army was between Catterick and Brough where it exercised no influence whatsoever on the course of events.

On 26th May, Brereton wrote from Withington, where he had set up his headquarters, to Lord Fairfax.

> "According to ye Orders of ye Comittee of both kingdoms and your Ldspp there are already drawne to ye Rendezvous at Barlow More the Cheshire horse, Colonell Duckenfields and part of Colonel Ashtons

Regiments of foote but ye Lancashire Horse and Colonell Holland's Regimt are not yet marched thither from ye service against Latham.

.........The number hereof that may depended upon wee believe will not amount to much above 1000 foote and fower of five hundred horse and Dragoons wch are only ye Cheshire horse."

It certainly appeared during those few days that Didsbury was to be the scene of an armed struggle, but such was not to be. The King advanced as far north as Market Drayton which he reached on 20th May. On 22nd May he resumed his march. At that time, as we have seen, Brereton's army had pulled away from Chester and had the King wished he could have linked up with his supporters there with little trouble. But since his main purpose in the north was to raise the siege he considered it accomplished when he heard that Brereton had drawn off. Further, he became aware that Sir Thomas Fairfax (Lord Fairfax's son) and Cromwell were converging on his old headquarters at Oxford with a large army and decided to march into the Midlands to draw them away. Passing through Burton upon Trent and Ashby-de-la-Zouche he reached Leicester, which he took by storm on 31st May. Two weeks later he was defeated at Naseby in the greatest and most decisive battle of the war.

What part, we may ask, did the rendezvous on Barlow Moor play in forcing the King to change his plans? Besides the desire to relieve Oxford he probably had another reason for turning into the Midlands. He believed that the northern forces of Parliament were stronger than he had been told. Writing to the Queen on 14th May, from Droitwich, during his march north he said:-

"I am not very confident that their Northerne Forces are, but except they are much stronger than I am made beleeve."

At some stage during his march he must have been made aware of the rally on Barlow Moor, for writing to the Queen again, this time from Stone, on 23rd May, the very day after that fixed for the rendezvous, he observed:-

"I fynde (most assuredly) that all the Rebelles Armys ar gathering together Northeward."

Consequently it may have been that he formed a completely false mental picture of a large army waiting to meet him on the Mersey, an army from which he felt compelled to turn aside. Three years of war had told on his strength but, had he known it, the forces under his command outnumbered those on Barlow Moor several times over. He could easily have brushed aside Brereton's force and dealt separately with Leven further north. There would then have been no Parliamentary army west of the Pennines to prevent him from linking up with Montrose. Instead he marched right into the jaws of his enemy until events caught up with him at Naseby. What a chance he missed!

On 30th January, 1649, Charles I stepped onto a scaffold overlooking

Whitehall and was beheaded, but England had not yet seen the end of the struggle between Roundhead and Cavalier. More was yet to come, and Didsbury saw its share.

In 1651, Charles's son, the future Charles II, moved down from Scotland with an army of Scots but was routed by Oliver Cromwell at the Battle of Worcester on 3rd September. His followers then tried to make their way back to Scotland in relatively small groups. All that is known about Didsbury's part in the story was contained in a letter written from Congleton, Cheshire, a few days after the event.

"Honoured Sir,
    On Thursday last there marched by out Town about 1000 of the routed Scots, who rendezvoused on Cangleton Moor, there taking up their quarters for the most part of that night, lying in their close order; but about 3 of the Clock in the morning, Major Gibson (a Countrey Gentleman) with about 300 Club men and others allarmed them which the enemy perceiving, indeavoured to make good his drawing off; but by the great forwardness and gallantry of the said Major he fel on with his men in their Rear, killed about 300, and took about 100 prisoners with little losse: for indeed so great is the spirit of fear amongst them that 10 men will chase 100. the rest of the enemy escaped; but we hear since are taken. On Fryday morning, another party consisting of about 500, marched by us, but the Countrey pursued them so close that the enemy were forced to face about, and dispute the place which conflict lasted for the space of half an hour, till at last the Countrey men fell in with their Clubs, Sythes and but end of Musquets, and totally routed them killing about 60, took divers prisoners of quality: amongst the rest Col. Hamilton, Sir William Hart and Collonel Hulmes (son to the Lord Hulmes) are taken. Having secured the prisoners, we farther pursued the enemy and about Diddesbury overtook them, where we killed, took and totally routed the whole party, with the losse of 11 men, so that now (blessed be God) most of the enemies of this Common-wealth, that got off from the first at Worcester, are all killed and taken: but Charles Stuart their Captain general hath again narrowly escaped, and out run them all, being habited in a mean Apparel, with only four men to attend him: he is gone towards Scotland with a great and pannick fear, by reason of the disaffection of the Countrey towards him, for in divers places where he came, the Inhabitants rose both against him and his followers, and fell upon them with their Clubs, and at Diddesbury he was constrained to force his passage through the midst of 40 Club men, who laid at him with their Clubs and yet could not bring him to the dust. However there is all dilligence used for the waylaying and intercepting him before he gets over Tweed. In many places where he came, where the people were gathered together he used these expressions, Good people, take commiseration on him, who is your true & lawful King, but words took these little impression in their hearts, for they made a generall resistance throughout all parts and unanimously declared against him and his followers, for

which, I doubt not, but they wil have a rich reward of mercey with God, etc."

The allusion to Charles II being in Didsbury was completely false. At just about that time he was hiding in an oak tree at Boscobel, but it is known that among his supporters was a tall young man whom the Roundheads believed to be the King until he was captured.

What became of the bodies of those that were slain? The parish register of Didsbury did not mention them and unfortunately no entries were made in the registers of St. Wilfrid's, Northenden, at that period, because of the troubled times. Yet members of the Didsbury Golf Club point to a slight mound, so low that it is almost invisible, at the end of the second fairway. Close inspection shows that it is shaped like a cross. Some of the older members recall having been told that there used to be a stone on the mound which bore an inscription to the effect that Scots were buried there. They recall also having been told that the Scots were killed in Cromwellian times.

Chapter V
THE YOUNG PRETENDER

The passage, in December, 1745, of the army of Charles Edward Stuart, otherwise the Young Pretender, otherwise Bonnie Prince Charlie has been referred to as Didsbury's most stirring event. In fact it must, in itself, have been no more spectacular than the passing of the army of Prince Rupert, the rally of Sir William Brereton's troops on Barlow Moor or the skirmish near Northenden Ford. It was, moreover, a brief episode, probably taking up no more than a couple of hours. But it was well documented, and it is possible to reconstruct an almost perfect account of what occurred. As was only to be expected the facts have been adorned with legends and we must endeavour here to sort out legend from history.

The Jacobite connections of the local landed gentry appear to have been strong. Indeed it is said that a group of Jacobites made a practice of dining at the Bridge Inn, Jackson's Boat, which stands on the river bank at the extreme end of Hardy Lane, Chorlton-cum-Hardy. After the meal it was their custom to place a bowl of water on the table, when every member of the company would hold his glass over the bowl and drink "the King". On one occasion a guest observed "This is not the toast I expected to be drunk here". "Tush" was the reply, "are we not drinking the King over the water?"

Manchester began to take practical steps against the invasion on 19th October, 1745, even before the Scots had passed their own border. On that date the constables sent out warrants to the outlying hamlets, of which Didsbury would have been one, summoning the militia to muster on 1st November. The Didsbury militia paraded in Manchester with the rest, but the call was either a false alarm or a rehearsal since they appear to have dispersed, being summoned a second time on 12th November. On that day three companies of foot soldiers and one troop of cavalry mustered and took up quarters in the town under the direct orders of Lord Derby, the Lord Lieutenant. They were joined next day by two more companies from Blackburn and on 19th October by another two companies. The men, being only part time soldiers, did not have uniform and in order to identify them in battle each man was given a cockade.

Thus equipped the militia waited to receive the highlanders. By 25th November news reached Manchester that the rebels were at Lancaster. The militia had then been under arms for nearly a fortnight and the constables sent out warrants to the hamlets to bring in fourteen days pay.

Next day the Scots were at Preston and something approaching a panic descended on Manchester. There was seen a sight which two hundred years later became all too common on the continent of Europe, the flight from a city of civilian refugees in the face of an advancing army. So general was the desire to evacuate that even the prisoners were released from the House of Correction to flee from the faceless terror approaching from the north. At about this time also the bridges over the Mersey at Stockport, Stretford, Barton and Warrington were destroyed to impede the rebel advance. By 27th November Beppy Byrom observed in her diary that there were not above four women hardly left in the (i.e. St. Ann's) Square.

Did the Manchester militia meet the invaders at the approaches to the town? Did they perish to a man in defence of their homes and loved ones? They did not. Their martial array ended in a manner worthy of a Gilbert and Sullivan operetta. On 27th November they were all discharged and sent home. At 3.p.m. next day, Thursday, 28th November, the town was occupied without opposition by a forward patrol of the Pretender's troops. This force consisted of two men in highland dress, one woman and a drum! Within hours they were followed by their cavalry.

Almost as soon as the rebels had arrived in Manchester in any appreciable numbers some of them marched round the town beating a drum and calling for volunteers. Five guineas were offered to every man who would join them. By 8.p.m. about 80 men had enlisted, each of whom was given a white cockade. Others of the invaders went round the town looking for billets for the force which was to come after them which numbered, they said, 10,000 men. This, as we shall see, was an exaggeration.

On Friday, 29th November, the main body arrived, not in a compact body but in relatively small groups and long drawn out columns which began to enter the town at 10 a.m. The Prince himself was at the rear of his army and did not arrive until 3 p.m. He immediately went to the quarters which had been found for him at the home of a Mr. Dickinson in Market Stead Lane, later known as Market Street. As a result of his sojourn there the house later acquired the nickname of the Palace. Palace Street marks its position to-day.

One of the invading army, a Yorkshireman, walked sword in hand to visit his sister who lived at Slade Hall which is still standing. This was the ancestral home of the Sydall family one of whom, Thomas Sydall, was among those who enlisted and paid a horrible penalty. The Sydalls were a

53

noted family of Jacobites. Thomas's father was among those executed in 1716 for giving aid to the Young Pretender's father.

The Scottish Army appears to have been made up as follows:-

Regiments	Colonels	Men
Lockyel	Cameron of Loch	740
Appin	Stewart of Ardshiel	360
Athol	Lord George Murray	1000
Canronald	Canronald of Canronald, Junior	200
Keppoch	Macdonald of Keppoch	400
Glenco	Macdonald of Glenco	200
Ogilvie	Lord Ogilvie	500
Glenbucket	Gordon of Glenbucket	427
Perth	Duke of Perth (and Pitsligo's foot)	750
Strowan	Robertson of Strowan	200
Maclauchlan	Maclauchlan of Maclauchlan	260
Glencarnick	Macgregor	300
Glengeary	Macdonald of Glengeary, Junior	300
Nairn	Lord Nairn	200
Edinburgh	J. Roy Stuard (and Lord Kelly's)	450
		——
		6287
In several small corps		1000
Horse (Lord Elcho) (Lord Kilmarnock)		160
Lord Pitsligo's horse		140
		——
		7587
		——

The army was also in possession of artillery and baggage, but the number is uncertain. One account said they had "13 field-pieces, some two, some four pounders; two carriages loaden with gunpowder and two sumpter horses". Another said "They had 16 pieces of cannon at Manchester, great numbers of cover'd waggons and near 100 horses laden" A third verson said they had 15 pieces of cannon and one mortar. It is said that as they passed through Kendal in Westmorland they had twenty horse drawn vehicles with them and if this was true then they would doubtless have had the same number at Manchester.

The advance of an army through strange country two hundred years ago was a very different business from what it is today. For one thing they would have little idea of the precise route. They probably had with them rudimentary maps, showing the main towns, so that when they were at Carlisle they would know that the road they wished to take was the one leading to Penrith and thence to Kendal. They probably knew enough about the rivers to know that at Preston they had to cross the Ribble, and at Manchester the Irwell. What they did not know was which of two alternative roads was the better, where the few bridges stood, where they would find marshes and where forests, and which routes led over rough country. Consequently it was necessary for them to advance some distance behind forward patrols which reconnoitred the country through which it was desired to pass and sent back the necessary information.

Having arrived at Manchester the Prince was faced with a considerable problem. He was aware that before him loomed the Mersey, as great an obstacle to his progress as any he had previously met. Reports had already reached the town before he arrived that the few existing bridges over the river had been destroyed. Having settled in the town on Friday, the 29th, he accordingly devoted the next day, which happened to be devoted in the Church calendar to St. Andrew, the patron saint of Scotland, to resting his tired troops and sending out patrols.

Of the fortunes of these patrols, which would undoubtedly be mounted, much was recorded and survives.

One party, it is known, went to Stretford, forcing labourers from Manchester to accompany them and taking with them ropes and nails with which to repair the bridge. Since they were bound for London the journey to Stretford was, of course, off their direct route. The purpose of their journey was probably to put into effect the oldest strategem of war, the creation in the minds of their enemies of a false idea of their true intentions. Even in Manchester members of the main army were apparently talking quite freely to the populace, some saying that they were bound for Derbyshire, others giving Chester as their destination, and others giving out that they were marching through Middlewich and Nantwich into Wales. These deceptions did not show a particularly high regard for the intelligence of the leaders on the other side, for it was clear that for the insurrection to succeed the Capital would have to be taken, the route to which lay through Macclesfield and Derby. In the event this was the route which the Scots took.

As well as wishing to create a feint the Scots would also have felt it necessary to have a small force to the west of the main body as a defence against the King's troops which they knew, or thought they knew, were in Knutsford and West Lancashire. Of an attack from the east they had little fear, for in that direction lay the Peak District which was much too wild and barren for an army to muster. On the departure of the main army from Manchester, therefore, a small body crossed the newly repaired bridge at Stretford, advanced to Altrincham, and from thence set out to rejoin the Prince at Macclesfield.

The road which the Scots wished to take led, of course, to Stockport and on the afternoon of Saturday, 30th November, ten of them arrived there to find the bridge destroyed. They stayed for about an hour. What they were looking for is obvious. Their army had, as has been mentioned, a number of guns and waggons which had to be got across the river at a place where they would not sink into a muddy river bed and where the powder could be kept out of contact with the water. Stockport was already a sizeable town, and the patrol must have taken note that the nearest trees large enough to repair the bridge were some considerable journey away from the spot where they were required. At that time the main road through Stockport was along the route which, to this day, is know as Old Road. In the town centre this road descended to the river down a slope which was so steep that it was eventually found necessary to place flights of steps down it. These still exist in Roman Road. There was a similar slope on the opposite bank. In those days the centre of the town was near Tiviot Dale and the bridge crossed the river at Bridge Street, to which it gave its name. Lancashire Hill, Wellington Road and Mersey Square were not created until very many years later. The heavy vehicles and artillery would have to be handled very carefully on the slopes going down to and up from the river for fear that they might career out of control into the water. All in all the place had little to recommend it as a crossing place for waggons and artillery, although there was no reason why infantry should not pass there.

Yet another patrol arrived at Didsbury. Of them the London Gazette of 4th September, 1745, contained the following report:-

"55 had the same day crossed the river at Gatley Ford to Cheadle two miles from Stockport and had returned directly after to Manchester by Cheadle Ford".

The route by which this patrol approached was probably along the road through Rusholme and Withington which we now know as Wilmslow Road. There is a legend, the truth of which it is not now possible to test, that as they passed the farmhouse where St. Paul's Rectory now stands, near the junction of Wilmslow Road and Palatine Road, they took away the meal which was being prepared by the lady of the house.

Didsbury was a very small and insignificant village in those days. The party would naturally have made for its centre which lay near the Church in the vicinity of the inns. Who can doubt that after their journey from Manchester they went into one or both of these inns for refreshment? The course of the Mersey lay only a few minutes ride to the south of them, and on making enquiries about the points where crossing could be made, they would have been told that there was no bridge between Stockport and Stretford, but that there was a ford at the bottom of Stenner Lane on the road to Northenden, a second at the end of the Millgate, now known as Millgate Lane, which led to Gatley, and a third where Wilmslow Road now crosses the river at the spot then known as Cheadle Ford. They would also have been told that if they were wishing to go to Stockport and Macclesfield then the road to Northenden would lead them out of their way. Consequently they set about exploring the other two, choosing first the ford at the end of the Millgate. The commencement of the Millgate was only a few yards from the inns, and as it seems possible that, at that time, it was a wider and more important road than the road to Cheadle, it may have presented the obvious first choice for exploration. Times indeed change, and so do places! Going down the Millgate they would have noticed that it ran for a considerable distance over very low lying fields which at that time of the year would have been sodden. The road itself, being the main road to Gatley, was probably in a worse state than the fields, having been churned up by the wheels of traffic. An army trying to move its heavy equipment over the road would have been faced with the problem of mud which became all too familiar to the British troops in Flanders in 1917. Arriving at Gatley Ford they probably noticed that no bridge-making materials were at hand. They accordingly crossed the river at that point and hurried to inspect the third crossing place at Cheadle Ford. We observe from the report that having arrived at that place they re-crossed the river and returned directly to Manchester. The reason for their immediate return to the main army is clear. They had found what they were seeking. Growing at the side of the river, near to the ford, were a number of huge poplar trees long enough to span the water. The road to the ford descended a gentle slope to the water's edge and there was another such slope on the Cheshire side. With the trunks of the poplar trees it would be possible to make a crude dam over which the artillery and waggons could be manhandled.

The army resumed its advance next day, Sunday, 1st December. All accounts of the departure of the Prince's army from Manchester agree that they took the road to Stockport. This was the road commencing at Ardwick Green which is now called Stockport Road. Beppy Byrom recorded in her diary that same day that the Prince himself went over Cheadle Ford, but a much more reliable version of his crossing was, no doubt, that contained in a letter written that day from Butley Ashe, two miles north of Macclesfield which went as follows:-

"About three this afternoon march'd by the Pretender's son at the head of two regiments of foot, one of which is called his; he marched all the way from Manchester and forded the river above Stockport, which took him up to the middle. He was dressed in a light plaid belted about with a blue sash; he wore a grey wig with a blue bonnet, with a white rose in it and it was observed that he looked very dejected. The bulk of his army were very ordinary, only his own regiment seemed to be picked and a tolerable appearance. Their advanced guard get into Macclesfield before the main body passed this place".

The writer of this letter must have had a first hand account of the crossing, very shortly after it took place, from men who had taken part in it. This Beppy Byrom could not have had since she remained behind in Manchester. Doubtless the Prince crossed the river near the site of Bridge Street.

It is known that the army advanced along the Stockport Road. But what of the artillery which is known to have crossed at Didsbury? There is no record that it left Manchester by any different route from the foot soldiers. Clearly what took place was that the entire army proceeded up the road which we now know as Stockport Road, which was the most direct route to Macclesfield and London. The intention was for the foot soldiers to wade across the river at Stockport. As the artillery and waggons reached Longsight they left the main column and, forking right, proceeded down Slade Lane which ran, as it still runs, into Burnage Lane. Advancing alone Burnage Lane, with Heaton Norris on their left, they arrived at the district now known as Parrs Wood. From there they proceeded to Cheadle Ford.

At the ford the rebels set themselves to making a bridge. All the horses in the district were commandeered and the villagers were compelled to assist. Fletcher Moss has expressed the opinion that the bridge built by the rebels was the one which collapsed in 1756. This is untrue. While records exist to show that a bridge on the same spot fell in 1756, it is known that that bridge was completed only a few weeks earlier. A cursory inspection of the river banks on either side of the existing bridge, will show that no poplar tree could possibly span the river at any appreciable height, and also be sufficiently strong over its entire length to support traffic. What must have happened was that the Scots threw the tree trunks into the water, filled the intervening spaces with stones and earth, and carefully trundled their artillery and waggons across. Consequently what they built was more in the nature of a dam than a bridge. It was rudimentary, it was by no means a masterpiece of engineering, but it was sufficient for its purpose. According to one account, the cavalry also passed at Cheadle Ford, but Beppy Byrom has put it on record that Lord Elcho's horse went past Baguley. This would suggest that some, at least, crossed the river at Barlow Ford which was near Barlow Hall. That the Prince's forces had informed themselves of the existence of that crossing is beyond question. Thomas Walley, one of the constables of Manchester at the time, recorded in his diary that an officer of the Scottish Army summoned him into his presence at 3p.m. on the day of the crossing and demanded a horse and a man to take him over the river there. In all probability the existence of the ford had been detected by one of the patrols the previous day.

The advance of the Prince's army continued as far as Derby where a Council of War was held. There had been hope that, as the advance continued, the army of highlanders would have been augmented by English Jacobites but such enlistments, while as we have seen they took place, were on such a paltry scale as to cause grave concern to the Prince's advisers. In view of these circumstances it was deemed prudent to abandon the march on London, return to Scotland, and meet the pursuing English army there. Much against his personal wishes the Prince agreed to this plan.

Consequently, on Friday, 6th December, the Scottish army began to retreat. The news of this development reached Manchester on Saturday the 7th, when a man from Leek arrived with a report that the rebels were once again in that town. The panic into which this information threw the town seems to have been absolute. So intense was the confusion that directly contradictory orders as to how to deal with the new crisis were issued. At first it was determined to make a stand and the bellman was sent round the town with a proclamation; "This is to give notice to all inhabitants of this town that they are desired to rise and arm themselves with guns, swords, pickaxes, shovels or any other weapons they can get, and go stop all the ends of the town to prevent the rebels from coming in for two hours, and the King's forces will be up with them". Within a very short time country people from the villages on the north side of the town came pouring in with a strange motley of home-made weapons. As was only to be expected, discipline was non-existent among them, for all their soldiery ambitions, and within a short time they had degenerated into a mob. Fearing that the town was about to be turned into a battlefield, one of the constables posted watchmen at Red Bank, which is still the name of a street near the commencement of Cheetham Hill Road, and at Newton Lane which is now known as Oldham Road, so as to prevent the mob from entering the town. Gone was now any desire to resist the Scots and the bellman was sent round the town with a second proclamation: "Whereas a tumultuous mob has been raised, etc., this is to desire that all the country folks will go to their own homes, and that everybody will lay down their arms and be quiet". Surprisingly enough the proclamation had its effect and the rabble disappeared without trouble, but some of them, under one Hilton, who had assumed the position of their leader, hurried to Cheadle Ford in an endeavour to remove the poplar trunks and so render it impossible for the Scots to get their artillery and waggons back across the river. Although the dispersal of the mob had taken place at the orders of the constables, they appear to have been parties to the destruction of the bridge, for which purpose they even supplied funds. It is not known for certain whether the mob succeeded in destroying the bridge. Beppy Byrom wrote in her diary that their expedition had been fruitless, but another account, written shortly after the event, has put it on record that they forced a party of the Scots to turn back and go through Stockport.

The Scots were back in Manchester at 2p.m. on Monday, 9th December. It is not properly known whether any part of their army passed through Didsbury in their retreat, but it is probable that they did for the same considerations would have applied as during their advance, making it impossible for the wheeled traffic to cross the river elsewhere.

On 10th December the following entry was made in the Didsbury parish register:-

"A poor man buried at Dids. found dead at Heton wn ye rebels past".

On the assumption that this entry was intended to suggest that the death of the poor man was connected with the passage of the rebels, it affords corroboration that Burnage Lane, which runs along the borders of Heaton Norris, was the route they took. It will be noted however that the man was buried after both the advance of 1st December and the retreat of the 9th. The entry is as likely to relate to the one event, as it is to the other.

It is not without interest to observe that although the parish register was kept, at the time, by the Minister, Rev. Robert Twyford, the entry just referred to was made by the hand of another. Perhaps Rev. Twyford had taken himself to a more tranquil part of the country. If so he had returned to Didsbury by 25th December.

Legends existed for many a long day that Duke's Hill, the ground in front of the Didsbury Hotel and the Old Cock, and Scotscroft, the land between Wilmslow Road and The Towers, derived their names from the Pretender's Army. We shall have occasion, in due course, to weigh the truth in these beliefs. Fletcher Moss also suggested that Famous Pits, the field at the corner of Burnage Lane and Parrs Wood Lane, also became "famous" because of some unspecified incident which took place there as the highlanders passed. In this case there is little evidence for the suggestion which, in all probability, was a product of wishful thinking.

Chapter VI

A JOURNEY THROUGH DIDSBURY

Let us, in our imagination, accompany a traveller through the village of Didsbury as it was at the end of the eighteenth century.

Approaching from Withington he would come along a road which had been in use for centuries. There exists an oblique reference to the highway from Wilmslow to Manchester in deeds executed in the middle of the thirteenth century, when it was referred to merely as the King's Highway. We now know it as Wilmslow Road.

According to modern standards the traveller would have found it in a deplorable state of repair. Since 1753 its maintenance had been the responsibility of the Manchester to Wilmslow Turnpike Trust. Created by Act of Parliament the turnpike trust was composed of local landowners and gentry and financed by tolls charged to passing traffic at Rusholme and Hurlbote, near Handforth. It was soon found, however, that traffic going south from Manchester had taken to using the roads through Levenshulme and Burnage, which we know as Slade Lane and Burnage Lane, to join the turnpike road in Didsbury, thus avoiding the payment of the toll at Rusholme. To prevent these evasions side-bars were eventually erected at the corners of Fog Lane and Parrs Wood Lane. Prior to the formation of the turnpike trust each township through which the road passed was expected to maintain its own stretch. No doubt the state of repair varied from township to township but in many cases the system meant that the roads were rutted dust tracks in the summer and quagmires in the winter.

We may assume that during the first few years after the creation of the turnpike trust conditions improved, but the road was not paved for some time and the state of most of the surface was so bad that it was virtually impossible for pack-horses, at that time a much used form of transport, to move along it. It was therefore found necessary, at some time in the eighteenth century, or earlier, to pave a narrow part of the road's width with stones so as to enable them to proceed. Paved paths such as this, known as horse causeways, were quite common in all parts of the country. The one to which we are referring stretched at least from the home of Rev. James Bayley, near the commencement of Cotton Lane, to Didsbury village. It is known to have been in existence in 1762.

With the phenomenal growth of Manchester as an industrial centre at the end of the eighteenth century, however, the amount of traffic on the main roads leading out of and into it must have increased enormously with the result that their condition probably took a turn for the worse instead of improving. This must have been especially true of the road through Didsbury, for it was part of the main highway from Manchester to London which approached from Rusholme and Withington and continued through Cheadle, Wilmslow and Congleton.

Our traveller would reach the northern boundary of Didsbury at the Ball Brook. This can still be seen in the open at the rear of Didsbury Court, disappearing into a culvert outside No. 58 Ballbrook Court. In those days it flowed in the open as far as the main road which crossed it by a bridge which, while it was not nearly as wide as the present Wilmslow Road, would certainly be wide enough to allow a coach or farm cart to pass. This bridge was known as Withington Bridge. On it was a stone, presumably to mark the boundary between the two townships. Even today the observant eye will see a semi-circular grey stone set in the wall of No. 626 Wilmslow Road. The carving on it has been much eroded by time and weather but it would seem to bear the date 1822, such being sufficient proof that it was not the original stone which our traveller would have seen.

Crossing Withington Bridge our traveller enters the township of Didsbury. On his left was a field called Near Meadow, now the site of Didsbury Court, Binswood and Fairfax House. In the Near Meadow there had formerly stood a cottage, the home of John Birch, a pavior, but this was demolished before the end of the century. In 1797 the Near Meadow was the property of Thomas Bailey, a Manchester merchant.

On the other side of the turnpike road, where Ball Brook Avenue now joins Wilmslow Road, stood a group of cottages which belonged to Miss Ann Broome. At least one of these had an orchard attached. Around them were fields known as ffar Meadow, Nar Meadow, Moorfield and Little Meadow.

Our traveller has now reached the crossroads where Fog Lane and Lapwing Lane now branch off Wilmslow Road. At this crossroads was set a stone which announced, rather erroneously, that the distance to Manchester was five miles. On the south side of what is now Lapwing Lane our traveller would have found two unusually large fields called Yannis's Twenty Acres and Clerk's Moor Fields, which stretched as far south as the road we now know as Barlow Moor Road. On this land there now stand Parkfield Road, Elm Road and Pine Road. This was the property of William Broome. There is no record of any buildings on these fields except, as we shall see, in the south-east corner. It was probably this land which was the camping ground of Prince Rupert's army in 1644 and the rendezvous of the Parliamentary armies in the following year.

Facing it on the other side of the turnpike road, and also belonging to William Broome, were a number of fields bounded on one side by the turnpike road and on the other by a hedge or a fence which exactly followed the present course of Beaver Road. These fields formed part of a farm known as Hughes's Tenement, the farmhouse of which seems to have been near the present position of the Church of St. Catherine of Siena. They were apparently enclosed off Didsbury Moor at such a late date that by 1798 they had not yet acquired districtive names, being known collectively as the Seven Intacks. A little later they acquired the rather picturesque names of the Fields before the Butchers, Dean's Garden, the Field next to Dean's, Red Knee, Fogg Lane Meadow, the Rough, the School Field, Old Frank's Intack and Rabbit Burrow.

The present School Lane was known as Warner's Lane. Near its junction with the Turnpike Road it occupied the same position as it does now but further down it took a very different course. Barlow Moor Lane, now called Barlow Moor Road, branched off opposite. Then, as now, there was a public house at the corner, but whereas the present building is known as the Wellington Hotel its eighteenth century predecessor was called the Grey Horse. It was one of Didsbury's three hostelries, the other two being the Ring o'Bells and the Cock, now known as the Olde Cock. Contemporary records also contain references to a tavern in Didsbury known as the Ball and Nimrod and this was probably an alternative name for the Grey Horse.

To the south of Barlow Moor Lane, on the west side of the turnpike road, was a row of buildings used by the local tradespeople as cottages cum shops cum workshops. This stretched as far as Crabb Lane, which was the eighteenth century name for Grove Lane, and was in the same position as the present row of buildings which includes a Chinese restaurant and Didsbury Police Station. We cannot be sure what trades were carried on or what goods were sold there, but in 1845 there was a beerhouse, a wheelright and a blacksmith and the same was probably the case when our traveller passed. Certainly the trades appropriate to a small country village would be represented. The buildings all stood in small gardens and appear to have been rather larger than the present shops, so that less than a dozen of them occupied the whole row. In this area the main road was known as the High Street. Legend has it that at some time the village stocks stood in front of the buildings.

Curiously enough there were no buildings on the other side of the road where Albert Hill Street, Oak Street and Elm Grove now stand. The fields on this site were known in the early nineteenth century as Pearl Croft, Smithy Croft and New Field, although those near the corner of Grange Lane appear to have been known previously as Nearer Goose Croft, Further Goose Croft Smithy Croft and Pingott. For some reason which has not come down to us these last named fields were absolved from the payment of tithes. Through the fields, along approximately the present course of

Oak Street, there flowed a small stream.

As we have seen Grove Lane was known as Crabb Lane. At the end of the eighteenth century cottages were being built on it which can still be seen to-day. It stretched as far as the present Osborne Street, acting as a means of access to the fields in the present position of Bamford Road.

Car Brow Lane, which was the name by which the present Ford Lane was known, joined the turnpike road where Dene Road joins Wilmslow Road now. That part of it which lay nearest to the main road has been completely obliterated by Dene Road which was laid out shortly before the Second World War. The field on the northern corner was known as Crabb Croft. In it was a building which was known as the Workhouse. While no evidence exists as to how it acquired this name it is not unreasonable to assume that it was the building in which the township bestowed its niggardly generosity on the impotent poor. Standing on land belonging to Mr. Robert Twyford, a Manchester merchant related to the minister, it appears to have been sold by auction in 1792. Its subsequent history is far from clear but after its demolition a house known as Didsbury Cottage was erected on the site which was for many years in the early nineteenth century the home of a Mrs. Ellen Markland. Landsdowne House stands in the same place today.

At the other corner of Car Brow Lane and the turnpike road were three small cottages with gardens belonging to Mrs. Ann Broome, which were occupied in 1783 by Samuel Smith, James Gaskell and James Cash. Behind them, on land now occupied by Ford Lodge and The Limes, was a field known as Shalcross Croft which was owned at the time by Mrs. Abigail Wood who inherited it from Thomas Hardy. In 1662 Thomas Brooke received this field from Sir Edward Mosley in exchange for some land fronting to Burnage Lane. It was part of their agreement that if Brooke did not like the house on Shalcross Croft after he and his wife had moved into it then Sir Edward was to give him £30 instead. He appears to have been satisfied with the house because he is known to have retained it.

If our traveller were now to cross the turnpike road and go down the road which we now know as Grange Lane he would come to cottages which had been the property, and one of them the home of Zechaeus Bancroft, who died in 1701, from whom they descended in succession to a family called Fildes. In 1793 Thomas Fildes sold the property to James Ward, the village schoolmaster, and for many years the collector of the township, who lived there until his death in 1822 when his son, James Walker Ward, who succeeded him as the schoolmaster, sold it to Mrs. Francis Barlow of Wilmslow. It was probably James Ward who demolished the existing cottages and built new ones with a barn and shippon attached. These buildings can still be seen. The main cottage, known as Moor Cottage, is the home of Miss Joyce Owen. Around the chimney stacks can be seen protruding bricks which show that originally the roof was of thatch. It is by no means the only building in Didsbury which still displays this feature.

The cottages which are now numbered 2, 4 and 6 Grange Lane were

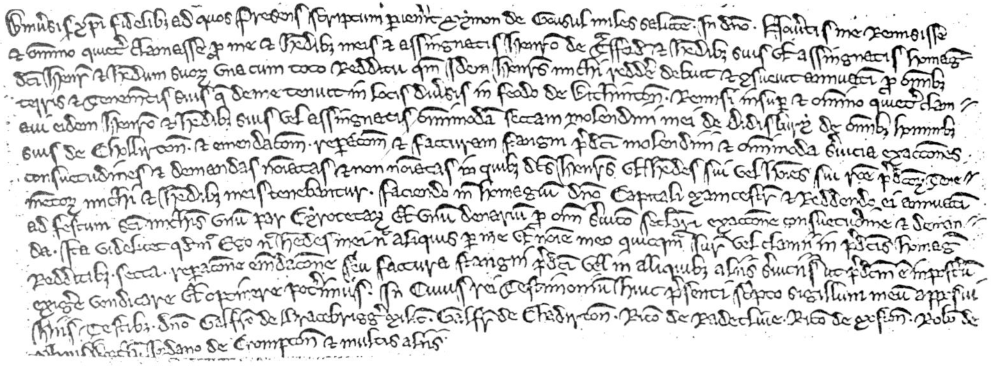

Plate 1

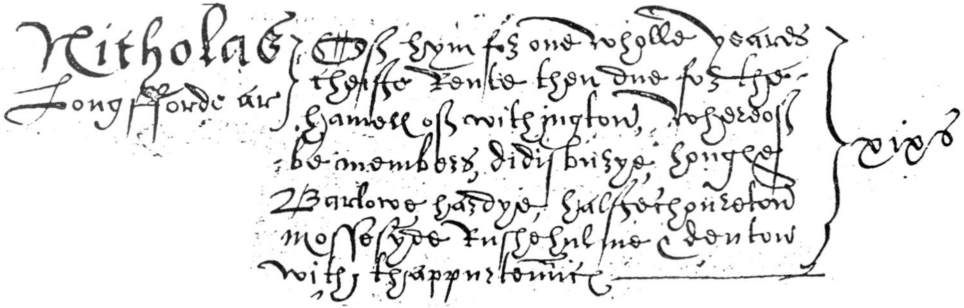

Plate 2

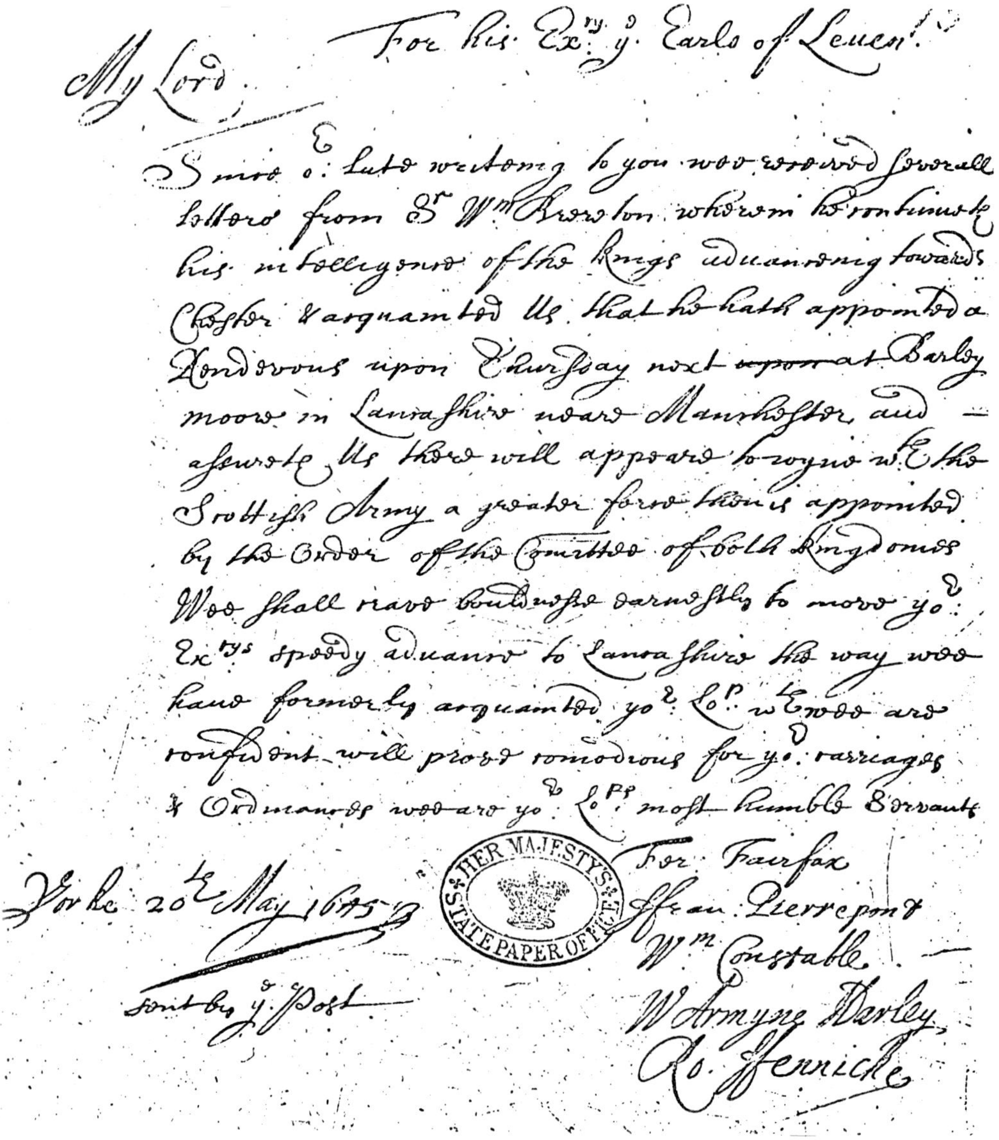

For his Exᵗʸ yᵉ Earle of Leuen:

My Lord.

Since oᵉ late writeing to you wee receiued seuerall
letters from Sᵣ Wᵐ Brewton wherein he continues
his intelligence of the Kings aduancing towards
Chester & acquainted Us that he hath appointed a
Rendevous upon Thursday next at Barley
moore in Lancashire neare Manchester and
asewrote Us there will appeare to ioyne wᵗᴴ the
Scottish Army a greater force then is appointed
by the Order of the Comittee of both Kingdomes
Wee shall neuer ceasse earnestly to moue yoᵉ
Exᵗʸˢ speedy aduance to Lancashire the way wee
haue formerly acquainted yoᵉ Lᵖˢ wᵗᴴ wᵉ are
confident will proue comodious for yᵉ carriages
& Ordnances wee are yoᵉ Lᵖˢ most humble Servants

Yorke 20ᵗᴴ May 1645   For Fairfax
                         Hen: Pierrepont
                         Wᵐ Constable
Sent by yᵉ Post   W: Armyne Darley
                         Ro: Jennison

Plate 3

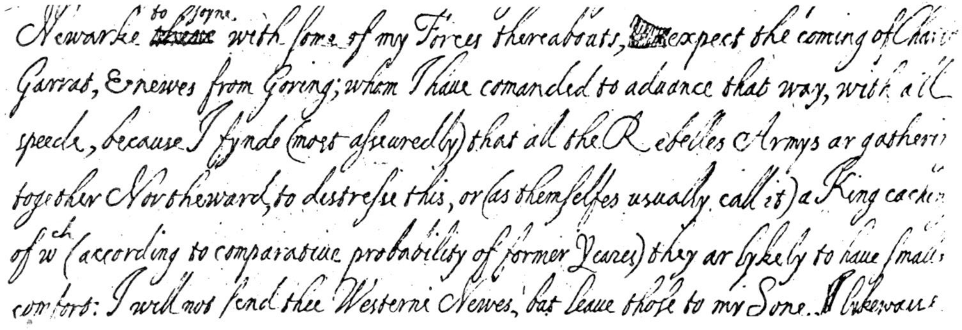

Newarke ~~there~~ to joyne with some of my Forces thereabouts, expect the coming of Charles Garrat, & newes from Goring; whom I haue comanded to aduance that way, with all speede, because I fynde (most assuredly) that all the Rebelles Armys ar gathering together Northeward, to distresse this, or (as themselfes usually call it) a King catching of wch (according to comparatiue probability of former Yeares) they ar lykely to haue small comfort: I will not send thee Westerne Newes, but leaue those to my Sone. I likewais

Plate 4

Honoured Sir,

ON Thurfday laft there marched by our Town about 1000. of the routed Scots, who randevouzed on Cangleton Moor, there taking up their quarters for the moft part of that night, lying in their clofe order; but about 3 of the Clock in the morning, Major Gibfon (a Countrey Gentleman) with about 300 Club men and others, allarmed them, whichthe Enemy perceiving, indeavoured to make good his drawing off; but by the great forwardnefs and gallantry of the faid Major, he fel on with his men in their Rear, killed about 300. and took above 100 prifoners with little loffe: for indeed fo great is the fpirit of fear amongft them, that 10 men will chafe 100. the reft of the enemy efcaped; but we hear fince are taken. On Fryday morning, another party confifting of about 500. marched by us, but the Countrey purfued them fo clofe, that the enemy were forced to face about, and difpute the place, which conflict lafted for the fpace of half an hour, till at laft the Countrey men fell in with their Clubs, Sythes, and but end of Mufquets, and totally routed them, killing about 60. took divers prifoners of quality: amongft the reft Col. Hamilton, Sir William Hart, and Collonel Humes, (Son to the Lord Humes) are taken. Having fecured the prifoners, we farther purfued the enemy, and about Diddesbury overtook them,
where

Plate 5

where we killed, took, and totally routed the whole party, with the losse of 11 men, so that now (blessed be God) most of the enemies of this Commonwealth, that got off from the fight at Worcester, are all killed and taken: but Charles Stuart their Captain General hath again narrowly elcaped, and out run them all, being habited in mean Apparel, with only four men to attend him: he is gone towards Scotland with a great and pannick fear, by reason of the disaffection of the Countrey towards him; for in divers places where he came, the Inhabitants rose both against him and his followers, and fell upon them with their Clubs, and at Diddesbury he was conftrained to force his pasfage through the midft of 40 Club men, who laid at him with their Clubs, and yet could not bring him to the duft. However there is all dilligence ufed for the way laying and intercepting of him before he gets over Tweed; In many places where he came, where the people were gathered together, He uf d thefe expreffions Good people, take commiferation on him, who is your true & lawful King, but words took thefe little impreffion in their hearts, for they made a generall refiftance throughout all parts, and unanimoufly declared againft him, and his followers, for which, I doubt not, but they will have a rich reward of mercy with God, &c.

From

Plate 6

LETTERS from Lancashire, Cheshire and Staffordshire, of the 30th past, bring Accounts, that about 200 of the Rebels had that Day come to a Pass three Miles from Manchester, leading to Knotsford, and had made a Sort of Bridge over the River, by filling it with Trees that they had fell'd, and had advanced to Altringham: That 55 had the same Day crossed the River at Gatley Ford to Cheadle, two Miles from Stockport, and had returned directly after to Manchester by Cheadle Ford: That 10 had crossed the Ford at Stockport that Afternoon, staid there about Half an Hour, gave out that they should bring a large Body of Forces to Stockport that Night, and that they had inlisted great Numbers of Men at Manchester, to which Place they returned. They had 16 Pieces of Cannon at Manchester, great Numbers of cover'd Waggons, and near 100 Horses laden. They talk'd differently about the Route they intended to take; some giving out they should march forthwith to Chester, and others into Derbyshire. The same Day 200 were at Warrington; two of whom, who had crossed the River, were seized by the Liverpool Soldiers, hand-cuffed, and sent to Chester.

Letters of the 1st Instant say, that several Parties of the Rebels had crossed the Mersey at different Places upon the 30th at Night, and early in the Morning of the 1st Instant, and were marching by different Routes towards Macclesfield. The Horse and Artillery passed at Cheadle Ford. The Bridges were made of Trees (chiefly Poplars) fell'd for that Purpose, and Planks laid across; and all the Country People that could be found, were compelled to assist them in it. They press'd or rather took away all the Horses they could meet with about Manchester,

[Price Two-Pence.]

Plate 7

248

Didsbury Township continued from page 180

1796

Oct. 19 To Daniel Worsley & Joseph Gordin Constables
         & 9 Assistants taking Smith, Rowley & Sergent
         in Custody all Night, paint & Shant & Beer   £3.0
    27   for Geo Rumboldown Water   £2.0.0 11.9
         eating in the morning   1.6

Nov. 8   To Daniel Worsley & Jos. Gordin Constables & 9 Assistants
         watching the Bond to take from Michaef had
         from him Beer 4/3, tobacco 1, Gin & Ale & Rum 9/8 20 6.6
    7   Didsbury Constables to a Letter paid for   3.3
    8   do.   do.   to do   3.3

15   1797 Received of Danl. Roberts Constable in July   £0.18.3
                                                  Settled

Didsbury Hotel and old Cock Inn.   Didsbury.

Plate 9

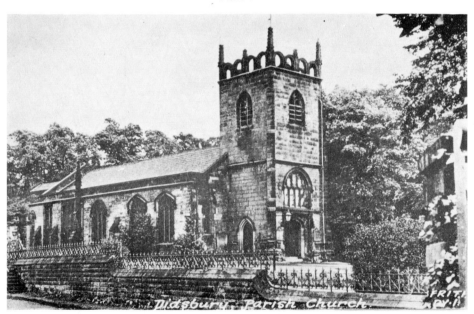

Didsbury Parish Church.

Plate 10

also the property of the Fildes family. They were in the ownership of that family as early as 1752 and as late as 1845, In all probability they were among the premises which the family inherited from Zechaeus Bancroft.

Adjacent to Thomas Fildes's cottages, on land now occupied by Viceroy Court, our traveller would have seen what must have been a large and well appointed house which was owned by Robert Feilden and occupied by Mrs. Hannah Broome, a member of the family to which his mother had belonged. Attached to the house there was an orchard and a field known as the Car below the Orchard. At the beginning of the nineteenth century a more imposing mansion was built there called Didsbury House and the older buildings converted into stables.

In later years Didsbury House became known as the Manor House, a name which gave rise to popular belief that Didsbury had been a manor in its own right, governed from that spot. This belief may have gained some erroneous support from the fact that Robert Feilden had arrogated to himself some of the functions of the lord of the manor, such as the privilege of nominating the village schoolmaster. He may even have laid claim to the lordship, but he had no title to it and there was no substance in the belief that the house was a manor house.

It is a matter of the greatest regret that very little is known of the early history of Broome House. The land on which it stands was known as the Croft behind the House and Piggott's Croft. The latter named field, at least, had formerly been part of the Didsbury estates of the Bamford Hesketh family and appears to have belonged to William and Catherine Tatton, of Wythenshawe Hall, in the early part of the eighteenth century. The name of the first named field shows that there was also a house, but nothing is known of it. It is also known that Broome House, which judging by its appearance was built at approximately the time that our traveller passed by, was for some time the home of Rev. John Gatliff who was minister of Didsbury from 1807 to 1840. It was also owned, for many years, by Hugh Hornby Birley, who was present at the Peterloo Massacre in 1819, as a Major in the Manchester Yeomanry.

Sandhurst Road probably originated as a cart track, giving access to and from the turnpike road to the farm which stood where the Provincial Laundry now stands at the bottom of Whitehall Road.

Our traveller has now reached the elegant mansion house which in its day must have been the architectural pride of Didsbury; a building known by the curious name of the Pump House, although why it got that name we do not know. It stood, and indeed it is not untrue to say that it still stands, on the site of the Didsbury College of Education.

On this same site there originally stood the house of Didsbury's very first owner-occupier. It was the home and property of Thomas Walker who died in 1602 or 1603. Shortly after his death the following entry was made in the records of the Manchester Court Leet:-

> "6th October 1603. The Jury dothe fynde that Thomas Walker of Didisburye ys depted since the last Courte leete but who is his heire we certenlye know not."

65

Thomas Walker, who was listed as a freeholder of the county in 1600, was probably the son of John Walker of Didsbury, who died in 1592 or 1593, and who was probably also the owner of the property. During the Civil War the house was the property of Lawrence Walker, who was one of the garrison of Wythenshawe Hall when it was besieged.

The premises remained in the possession of the Walker family until the middle of the eighteenth century, when they appear to have been sold to Richard Broome and John Broome by Samuel Walker, a Didsbury tanner. In 1785 Richard and John Broome sold them with a great deal of neighbouring property to William Broome who, like his father before him, was probably the steward of the Manor of Withington. It appears to have been he who demolished older buildings on the site and erected the Pump House.

William Broome died in 1780, but his son William Broome J.P., who died in 1810, continued to live in the Pump House. After his death it was inherited by his daughter, Maria Parker, who was the wife of Colonel John Parker, of Sharston.

In 1841 the Pump House was purchased by thirty-two Methodist trustees who added voluminous wings at each side, and in later years an extension at the rear. The entire building was also faced with stone, but the Pump House was never demolished and a visitor to Didsbury College of Education to-day can see the entrance hall with its elegant pillars and sweeping staircases and balustrade exactly as William Broome knew it and as our traveller would have seen it

To add to the grandeur of the Pump House was a fish pond, immediately opposite its front door, on the opposite side of the road. This was apparently made artificially by William Broome, the younger, in or about 1786 in a field called the Meadow or Carr, which later became known as the Croft covered with Water, and later still as Fish Pond Meadow. At the beginning of the nineteenth century there were also two cottages in this field occupied by Joseph Mason and Mrs. Walker. It may be because of this lady that the field on which the Didsbury clinic now stands became known as Walker's Croft. Other adjacent fields were known as the Great Croft and the Little Croft.

The Meadow or Carr sloped down to the flat land which now accommodates the Simon Playing Fields. At the bottom of the slope was a quick fence. Adjoining it on the far side of this fence, that is to say on the flat land, was a field called Thornhill's Carr which derived its name, no doubt, from John Thornhill, a Stretford man, who held it in lease in the middle of the eighteenth century.

Adjoining the Meadow or Carr, on the south side, our traveller would have found a substantial mansion house called Town's End or Yannis's Farm, adjoining which were two fields called the Croft and Shawcross Field. They were, of course, on the site of Philip Godlee Lodge. At the time the traveller passed the house it was the home of Ann Broome, daughter of Richard Broome, a Manchester attorney, first cousin of William Broome J.P. of the Pump House and aunt of Robert Feilden. The

66

holding appears to have been known as Town's End in the seventeenth century when a group of cottages stood there. It became known as Yannis House, Yannis's Farm or merely Yannis's at some time before 1734 and thereafter, until the end of the eighteenth century, it appears to have been known by these names as well as by its older name. It was at that time in the occupation of John Hulme. The name Yannis's Farm was derived from the Yannis family, who flourished in Didsbury in the reigns of Charles II and James II and then disappeared. There is no evidence that they lived at the farm although we may assume that such was the case.

To this day there stand two cottages in the grounds of Philip Godlee Lodge fronting on Wilmslow Road. One of them is occupied by the Coffee House Restaurant. They also bear signs of having had thatched roofs and we may be sure that our traveller would have seen them.

To the south of Philip Godlee Lodge there stands the Old Parsonage and Olde Cock Hotel. Fletcher Moss wrote much of the Old Parsonage, which was his home, as he did of the whole village, which he loved. Yet his account of the history of the house was neither exhaustive nor accurate.

While we know little of the history of the place we do know that it was not the traditional home of the ministers, as Fletcher Moss fondly imagined it to have been, although John Bradshaw, who was minister during the Civil War, lived somewhere in the immediate vicinity. It is true that in 1647, at the end of the Civil War, a house was set aside for the use of the minister and that the people of the village entered into an agreement for his maintenance. A draft of this agreement was preserved in the Church although the original has been lost. One clause read as follows:-

> "That the messuage and tenement assigned to the use of the ministr of the said church for the tyme beinge shall bee valued and accompted at the rate of tenne pounds p annu (towards the said XL Li p annu) consideringe the tymes and that Mr. Clayton is a single man & soe cannot husband it to advantage."

It will however be seen that this interesting passage does not contain the slightest evidence that the house assigned to the use of the minister was on the site of the Old Parsonage. Even if this was the case it is known that the ministers did not live there in the eighteenth century. Francis Hooper (Minister, 1721-1726) was the owner of Lum Farm and probably lived there. The farm stood at what is now the junction of Spath Road and Mersey Road. Robert Twyford (1726-1746) is known to have lived in a house somewhere near the present position of Broomcroft Hall, although we cannot be certain of its exact site. His son, William Twyford (1746-1795), probably lived in the same house. John Newton (1795-1807) lived in a house at the corner of the turnpike road and the Millgate which he built when he took up his appointment. Its site now forms part of the tennis courts in Fletcher Moss Park. John Gatliffe (1807-1840) lived at Broome House. Indeed the only period during which the Old Parsonage is known to have been the home of a clergyman was between 1829 when the curate, Rev. Sam Newall, lived there and 1850 when the rector, Rev. W.J. Kidd left to take up residence in Didsbury Park.

Almost the only certain historical fact known about the Old Parsonage in the eighteenth century is that at the end of that century it was part of the Didsbury estate of the Bamford Hesketh family. Like Broome House it appears to have been inherited by that family from John Davenport of Stockport. Prior to him the owners were the Tatton family of Wythenshawe Hall. Yet in deeds of the Bamford Heskeths, relating to their Didsbury estates, executed in 1761, no mention was made of a parsonage, nor, for that matter, was mention made of the Cock Inn. There was, however, a reference to a building called the Ash House, which was at that time in the occupancy of William Hesketh. It would seem, although we cannot be certain, that the Ash House was the eighteenth century name of either the Old Parsonage or the Cock Inn. Indeed it may have comprised both for they stood very close together and it is known that at some time in the past they were joined to each other.

In the middle of the seventeenth century the Ash House was in the occupation of Thomas Walker.

Only the central part of the Old Parsonage is original and even that has been much altered and restored in modern times. The high rooms at each end were added by Rev. Newall in the early part of the nineteenth century. In one of the internal doorways is a stone, set into the floor, clearly a doorstep leading in from the garden, which shows that the building must have been enlarged. The same doorway shows the marks of huge iron hinges of the type which were used on external doors in bye-gone days.

No more is known of the history of the Olde Cock than is known of that of the Old Parsonage. We do not know when an inn first appeared on that spot, or when it assumed its name, but we do know that as early as 1590 a family lived in Didsbury under the name of Blomeley alias Cocke. The curious custom by which whole families acquired aliases under which they were known for several generations, though now unknown, used to be quite common in Didsbury two or three centuries ago. In many cases the aliases were derived from the places at which the families lived. Thus the family of Blomeley alias Lowerhouse is known to have lived in a building, or perhaps a district, known as the Lowerhouse, which was certainly in Didsbury, although we do not know precisely where. The family of Ridings alias Tipping was originally known as Ridings, and is known to have farmed a holding, where Cavendish Road is now, which included a field called the Tipping Croft. During the Civil War Robert Blomeley alias Boate lived near Cheadle Ford, a spot known, at that time, as the Boate. Even more obvious examples of the same custom were to be found in the names of Ridings alias Timperley, Goddard alias Hadfield and Brown alias Padfield. We cannot overlook the possibility that the existence of the name Blomeley alias Cocke, at the end of the sixteenth century, revealed the existence of the inn under its traditional name.

In front of the Old Parsonage, immediately adjacent to the lane, even then known as Stenner Lane, but also as Car Lane, and later as Spring Hill Lane, our traveller would have found a small building which survived well into the nineteenth century. Fletcher Moss believed that this had been the home of the parish clerks, and that it had been used as a school. If this was so the school must have been the Sunday school which is known to have been in existence in 1803.

Our traveller would, of course, now be in the heart of the ancient village. The village green was the open space, now used as a car park, in front of the Didsbury Hotel and the Olde Cock. There is no reason to doubt that cock fighting and bull baiting were carried on there. It was also the focal point of the wakes which took place on 5th August each year when it would be covered with booths and side-shows. A bonfire was held there every year on 5th November and on 28th January, 1793 the effigy of Tom Paine, the author of "The Rights of Man" was burned there.

At the time our traveller made his journey the green was known as Duke's Hill or Duke's Hillock. There is a legend that this name originated in an incident which took place when part of the army of the Young Pretender passed through Didsbury in 1745. The Duke of Perth, who was one of the commanders of the army, is said to have climbed a small mound on the green and addressed the people of the village.

Fletcher Moss strongly favoured this explanation. In its favour, it must be said that the Duke of Perth was indeed in command of the baggage train, which was the section of the army which crossed the Mersey where Cheadle Bridge now stands. Consequently it may be taken for granted that he himself passed through Didsbury. The Scots are known to have passed on the morning of 1st December, which happened to be a Sunday, when the village green would have been full of people who had come to the chapel not only from Didsbury but from Withington, Burnage, and Heaton Norris also. They were anxious to recruit volunteers from the districts through which they passed and it is by no means unlikely that their commander would have made use of the presence of a sizeable audience to make a recruiting speech. Hence the legend may have a basis of truth as most legends have to a greater or lesser extent.

On the other hand there is always a temptation to romanticise about such events and to allow the wish to be father of the thought. The possibility exists that Duke's Hill lent its name to the family of Blomiley alias Dukes, who were living in the village under that name as early as 1592. Clearly this explanation, if true, would negate the other.

The inn which stood where the Didsbury Hotel stands today was known as the Ring o' Bells, although it later acquired the name of the Church Inn. If our traveller has stayed in the village for any length of time he would have realised that this was the centre around which the administrative and social life of Didsbury revolved. Here the people of the township met to elect constables and to draw up lists from which the collectors, assessors and surveyors of the highway were appointed. Here was a hall where such public meetings as there were took place, as when in

1800 the farmers of the district met to protest against a suggested toll on dung. Here the social clubs of the village such as the Didsbury Archers, the Didsbury Hunt, the Gentlemen Bowlers and the Didsbury Female Friendly Society, held their functions. Here a dinner was provided for working people at the price of 1/-, and luxurious meal for the gentry at 2/6. Here lodging accommodation, of a type which was not refused by the upper middle classes, was provided at 2/6 per night. Here also an occasional auction sale took place, although a more favoured venue for that purpose was the Bull's Head Hotel in Manchester.

If our traveller had explored the precincts of the Ring o' Bells he would have found the bowling green where it is today. The vacant space immediately at the rear of the buildings, facing the great east window of the church, was an orchard. In the grounds was a building called the Milkhouse, which was presumably where cows were milked, for as we shall see the innkeepers were farmers also. In all probability this was the same building as now houses the Toc. H. South Manchester Rugby Football Club.

The landlord of the Ring o' Bells, up to his death in 1790, was William Wood, who was also the parish clerk. His son, James, succeeded him as clerk, and another son, Thomas, succeeded him as landlord of the inn. James Wood died in 1805 and a few days later Thomas Wood wrote in his notebook "Self appointed clerk by Mr. Newton." How long the Wood family managed the inn we cannot tell, although they had certainly left it by 1821, but an entry was made in the Parish Register in 1645 among the burials as follows:-

"Thomas Wood of Didsbury alehousekeep   August 5."

On the assumption that Thomas Wood's inn was on the site of the Ring o' Bells this was the first reference to the place that has reached us.

It must not be thought, either, that being innkeepers involved only the sale of intoxicants. The Ring o' Bells had a reputation of being a high class eating house and was much patronised by the local gentry. It was also a shop where a wide variety of goods, ranging from farming implements to newspapers, could be purchased. In addition the landlords acted as transport contractors and were willing, for a fee, to move a crop of vegetables or a load of dung for a short distance.

The Woods were also farmers on a fairly substantial scale. They were the tenants of a farm of 13½ acres on part of which the inn stood. It appears to have extended along the west side of Millgate Lane, thus taking in the site of Fletcher Moss Park. It comprised fields called Turnip Field, ffarther Croft, Nar Croft, Whittle Croft, Nar Shawcross Car, Ffar Shawcross Car and Blomiley's Meadow. Also included were Wash Hole and Brown Half Acre which were on the site of Didsbury Refuse Tip. In addition the Woods were for a time tenants of Withy Ley, now known as Simon Playing Fields; Brown Dole near where the Didsbury Golf Clubhouse stands; Birches near where Kingsway now crosses the river; Famous Pits where the allotments now lie in Parrs Wood Lane and

Orchard Croft the location of which is unknown.

The church was, of course, and still is approached by a road passing between the two inns. At some uncertain time this road became known as the Gates of Hell, since many there were who turned off at either side, yet few passed between!

The church, or to refer to it more correctly, the chapel, would have appeared very different to our traveller from what it does to us. The churchyard was very much smaller than it is now. At the westerly end the line of the old wall can still be seen, the addition to the churchyard at that end being rather lower than the older part. The lane which now runs along the easterly end to Fernbank and Highbank has been moved to the east of its former position so that the churchyard could be extended to provide space for the Lych-gate.

Prior to 1770 the building was very much smaller than that which we know now. The east window was in a position approximately at the end of the present nave. The chancel was not as wide as the nave and the Mosley Chapel was not in its present position, although the Barlow family had a chapel on the north side of the building. Already, however, there was a gallery at the west end which had been erected in 1751.

In 1770 a new chancel, and presumably the Mosley Chapel also, were erected, followed about twenty years later by north and south galleries built along the entire length of the church. Our traveller would certainly have seen the present tower, although it did not then boast a clock. Erected in 1621 it is certainly the oldest existing structure in Didsbury. It is thought that the interior of the tower dates back to mediaeval times.

Inside the building the traveller would have found a small library and a bonded wooden chest which contained the churchwarden's accounts, the deeds of the village school endowment and a variety of other items ranging from an attendance register of the Withington Court Leet to a copy of Lady Ann Bland's will. Happily these have been preserved.

The wealthier families of the district occupied private pews which were their own property to be bought and sold. The ownership of a pew was frequently attached to landed estate and passed to the new owner when the land was sold.

The churchyard would, of course, be full of gravestones but, alas, the older ones have all been removed, except a few, such as the one which leans against the east end of the church, and two more in the small vestry on the south side of the nave. It has already been shown how the churchyard was so much smaller than in modern times. Since no less than 7,649 bodies were interred in it between 1562 and 1757 alone it is clear that the removal of gravestones (and bodies) must have been a fairly regular occurrence. Fletcher Moss never tired of pointing out that there had been a path known as Dark Lane, running from the south-east corner of the churchyard, across Millgate Lane, and on to a point in Wilmslow Road just north of the bridge. As he affirmed that this path was stopped up during his lifetime we are not in a position to contradict him, but it was not shown either on the Tithe Map of 1845 or the 6" Ordnance

Survey Map of 1848 and consequently it could not have been of great importance.

Doubtless there were, at all times since the foundation of the church, small cottages on the high land which now accommodates Fern Bank and High Bank, as well as other places in the immediate vicinity of the village green, although their exact positions have not come down to us. It is said that there were a few small thatched cottages where the lych-gate now stands. If this is true they had certainly disappeared by 1821.

The ground drops sharply behind Fern Bank and High Bank. At its lowest level there was, in the early part of the nineteenth century, a timber yard which belonged to the Peacock family. If this was not yet in existence at the turn of the century it must have been founded shortly afterwards.

As we have seen, our traveller would have had Wood's farm on his right as he left the village green and continued along the turnpike road. The land now occupied by the tennis courts was known as the Shooting Butts and was, as that name suggests, a range where archery was practised. It was provided by the Woods for the entertainment of their customers in much the same way as they provided the bowling green. It is known to have been used for archery in 1792. In 1795 however the newly appointed minister, Rev. John Newton, built his house at the corner of Millgate Lane, then known as the Millgate, and the turnpike road and at that time, or very shortly afterwards, the Shooting Butts, appear to have been absorbed in his garden. It has been suggested that the history of the archery range goes back to the reign of Henry VIII, when it was made obligatory for every village to provide facilities for archery practice, and for all that is known to the contrary this may be true.

Opposite the opening of the Millgate was a group of cottages belonging to Thomas Whitelegge, which remained in his family for many years, after which they became the property of the minister, Rev. John Newton. They were subsequently demolished. The Grove now stands on the land which they occupied.

The Clerk's Meadow appears to have been the eighteenth century name for the field on which Nos. 811 and 813a Wilmslow Road now stand Next to that, at what is now the junction of Didsbury Park and Wilmslow Road, was a field called Sparrow Greave. These fields belonged to William Broome of the Pump House and were, no doubt, part of his private grounds.

At the rear of the Pump House, stretching from the Clerk's Meadow and Sparrow Greave to the lane which we now know as Sandhurst Road, was a field called the First Paddock which had been formed at or towards the end of the eighteenth century by the amalgamation of two fields called the Hemp Croft and the Long Croft. These were the remains of the fields on part of which the Pump House had been built. In the seventeenth century the Hemp Croft had been known as the Impcroft and adjacent to it, at that time, had been a field called the Browe. Didsbury Park now stands on the same land. To the east of the First Paddock were two more large fields called the Middle Paddock and the Further Paddock, which lay along the turnpike road as far as the present position of Parrs Wood Omnibus Depot, and stretched also beyond the position of Ruabon Road. These were formed by the amalgamation of Wood's Townfield, Wood's Illbeard, Clerk's Illbeard, the Croft, the Salt Rooks and Walker's Illbeard. They were also the property of William Broome and like the Clerk's Meadow and Sparrow Greave were probably in his occupation also.

On the south side of the main road the field which is now the front grounds of the Shirley Institute was known, even at the time our traveller saw it, as Scotchcroft. There can be little doubt that it acquired this name from the presence of the Scottish Army in 1745. The site of the building now know as The Towers and the land in the immediate vicinity near Parrs Wood Road were divided into an agglomeration of small fields called Flatt, Cock Croft, Nar Nan Bank, Middle Nan Bank, Ffar Nan Bank, Peas Croft, Hoady Bottom and Little Birch which belonged to Robert Feilden and were farmed, in 1783, by Samuel Thornley. Adjacent to these fields, on the east side, that is to say occupying the present positions of Didsbury Cricket Ground and Parrs Wood Railway Station, were the Croft, Car, Hoady Bottoms, Lower Hoady Bottoms, Nar Dole, Ffar Dole, Yannis New Field, Top Bank, Yannis Car, Croft Field, Nar Hoady Bottoms, Nearest but one Hoady Bottoms, Nearest but two Hoady Bottoms, and Ffarther Hoady Bottoms. These were also the property of Robert Feilden and were farmed in 1783 by John Hampson. The fields known as Hoady Bottoms, a name which eventually became changed to Heathy Bottom, lay exactly where Parrs Wood Road now lies. Here the mediaeval system of agriculture survived until the beginning of the nineteenth century and our traveller would have seen the land cultivated into strips as it had been for centuries. In Barcicroft the system survived even longer.

Not far from Hoady Bottoms the turnpike road was joined by the road from Stockport to Didsbury which we now know as Parrs Wood Lane, and further along as Didsbury Road. The point where the roads met was known as Three Lane Ends where there was a toll bar across the road from Stockport. At this junction also was the sixth milestone out of Manchester. This can be seen today in the garden of the Old Parsonage, whither it was moved by Fletcher Moss, who was an enthusiastic collector of historical items. It is fortunate for local history that he was so. His acquisitive instincts saved many an irreplaceable old document from destruction.

On his left the traveller would have seen the great mansion house, probably known even then as Parrs Wood, which was erected shortly before 1795 by William Boardman who subsequently became bankrupt. At the end of the eighteenth century it was the property of Richard Atherton ffarington about whom little is known except that he was a relative of Joseph Farington R.A. the artist, who died at Parrs Wood in 1821. The land which R.A. ffarington owned when our traveller passed was bounded on the north by the road from Stockport, on the west by the turnpike road, on the south by land now used as football fields near the river and on the east, at least approximately, by the boundary of Heaton Norris which now coincides with the boundary between Manchester and Stockport. He also owned a field on the west side of the turnpike road where the Gateway Hotel now stands.

Prior to its acquisition by William Boardman the land to the east of the turnpike road consisted in the main of two small farms. The one of these comprised a farmhouse and fields called the Greengate, the Further Mounthousend, the Pitshead and another field, also called the Greengate or Alexander Wood's Greengate. It was in the possession of Thomas Hardern. The other farm which consisted of a farmhouse and fields known as the Cockshut, the Great Birch fflat, the little Birch fflat was the property of William Broome and was occupied by John ffletcher. In addition to the two farms there was a holding of two fields called the Cockshut and the New Field which was in the occupation of John Birch, and also a cottage with orchards and a croft attached.

In the north easterly corner of his estate, that is to say on the land which now faces the mouth of Burnage Lane and through which the railway line runs, R.A. ffarington owned a piece of land called the Barlow Croft which had formerly been known as Bolt Gate Croft or Bout Gate Croft. He purchased this in 1799 from Samuel Hampson and John Rudd who were the executors of John Hampson, who lived at Bolton Wood Gate, that being the name of the farmhouse which is now No. 1002 Burnage Lane.

The field on the west side of the turnpike road, where there now stands the Gateway Hotel, has been known as ffletcher's or Bayley's Stoney Lands. In it had stood a cottage which was the home of John ffletcher who, as we have just seen, was the tenant of one of the farms on the east side of the road. The cottage was pulled down by William Boardman shortly before 1795 and, notwithstanding that it was separated from Parrs Wood by the road, the field was utilised as part of his gardens.

The land used as football fields between Parrs Wood and the river was made up of fields known as Moor Bank, the Moor Bank Meadow and the Patch, which were owned by Ann Broome, and the Great Meadow which was owned by Rev. James Bayley of Withington and Frances Bayley, his wife. All these fields were occupied by Thomas Rudd and John Rudd. In addition there was a field there called Meer Bank or Mear Bank which belonged to the Bamford Hesketh family.

Opposite these fields and standing on land now fronting the corner of Morningside Drive and Wilmslow Road, our traveller would have found Boathouse Farm, the property of Sir John Parker Mosley, at that time lord of the Manor of Manchester, and Henry ffielden who held it as trustees of Rev. James Bayley's and Frances Bayley's marriage settlement. The fields, which reached as far as Mellington Avenue and Gawsworth Avenue lie now, were called Margaret Acre, Dick Croft, Risings, Little Croft, Water Acre, Barncroft and Dick Acre. Lying across the site of Kingsway, near where it passes the Gateway Hotel, were Little Birch and Side Shutt. Also part of the farm was the site of the Galleon Swimming

Pool which was known as the Coppice. Boathouse Farm took its name from Cheadle Boat, as the river crossing was called, although it was also referred to as Cheadle Ford. As far as we can see several families, the Jacksons, the Chorltons, and the Blomeleys lived at the farm between 1608 and 1674. Henry Ridings was in occupation in 1720 and continued so until his death in 1727. A few years later we find that the occupier was Thomas Smith who was still in occupation in 1756. It was, of course, during Thomas Smith's tenancy that the place became famous as the spot where part of the Young Pretender's Army crossed the river in 1745.

Our traveller would have found the river spanned by a good and substantial bridge built by the turnpike trust in 1780. Having crossed it he would be in Cheshire and out of Didsbury, yet on his right, just a few yards from the road, was a field called Coppice Warth which was one of the four parts of Didsbury which lay south of the river. It was a detached part of Broad Oak Farm, owned by Ann Broome, and tenanted by James Rudd.

Thus ends the traveller's journey. Since crossing Withington Bridge he would have walked 1 mile 2 quarters and 433 yards along the turnpike road.

Chapter VII

A JOURNEY THROUGH DIDSBURY (Continued)

In his imaginary journey our traveller kept himself on the turnpike road, near to which most of the population of the township lived, and along which the fields were, or had been, very small and intensively cultivated. Let us now consider what he would have seen if he had explored the lanes leading off the main road.

Had he enquired for Fog Lane of a passer-by he would have had no difficulty in obtaining directions, as it had been known by that name since the end of the sixteenth century, and probably longer.

On the northern side of the lane, at the corner of Wilmslow Road, was a small slip of land belonging to Miss Ann Broome, known as Lane End. Also belonging to Miss Broome was the house, which still stands today and is known as Barfield Cottage, No. 1 Fog Lane. At the end of the eighteenth century this would have been thatched, and at that time it did not have its bay windows. It was occupied by the keeper of a toll bar, which lay across the lane just outside it. As we have already seen the Ball Brook crossed the lane here and flowed along the western boundary of the toll-house garden, as indeed it still does.

Lying to the north of Fog Lane, and bounded on the west by the Ball Brook, and on the east by a boundary now in the vicinity of Sussex Avenue, lay a number of fields which had some time previously been known as Smith's Tenement, after a family which had farmed it for generations. Fronting the lane a little further down from the toll bar was the farm house of this tenement, which was known as the Croft. On the other side of Fog Lane, on land which is now occupied by Willoughby Avenue, were other fields which were also part of Smith's Tenement, as was a narrow strip of land lying along the south side of the lane, almost as far as its junction with the main road.

By 1745, that part of Fog Lane Park which lies south of the stream, at that time known as the Intacks, had become part of the same holding as

Smith's Tenement. The whole was then owned by one Edward Hobson, who, in 1764, granted it to eleven trustees. The grant was upon the following trusts:-

> "...... towards teaching to read the English tongue write and cast accounts at or in any school now erected or hereafter to be erected in Audenshaw in the County of Lancaster such and so many poor children who for the time being shall dwell in the said Township of Audenshaw but not excluding other poor children and in paying the rent of such school or schools and the charges of maintaining and keeping the same in good repair as the trustees or the major part of them ... shall in their discretion think fit".

And we shall see, Didsbury had its own school with a not dissimilar endowment.

The district to the east of Smith's Tenement, which is now marked by the entrance to Fog Lane Park, was known as Little Heath, and was so described in the will of Sir Nicholas Mosley, made in 1612, although the same name was in use as early as 1587. The name is now recalled by Heath Place, which is a row of cottages fronting to Fog Lane near the entrance to the park. There was here a small group of houses, some of which appear to have been the homes of a family called Birch for several generations. As the Smiths gave their name to a tenement so did the Birches. Birch's Tenement now forms a large part of Fog Lane Park, near the gate leading to Old Broadway. It included fields called the Great Croft, the Little Croft and the Two Old Fields. At the turn of the century the tenement was owned by William Broome.

The area where Princes Avenue now stands was known as the Little Field, and was part of a holding which also included the site of Mereland Avenue, that part of the park which lies round the artificial duck-ponds and the site of Austin Drive, on the south side of Fog Lane. The macadamised path into the park lies roughly along the course of an old cart track called Cow Lane and the fields were known as Cow Lane Fields and Long Field. The history of this holding is not clear, but it seems to have been farmed by one James Blomiley in 1785.

Immediately north of the stream in the park were two fields called Little Heath, after the district in which they lay. They were included in a large purchase made by Samuel Egerton, of Tatton Hall, in 1758 from Richard Broome and John Broome, who were probably acting as intermediaries for Sir John Bland. At the end of the eighteenth century they were owned by Samuel Egerton's nephew, William Egerton, who was the grandfather of the first Lord Egerton of Tatton.

At what is now the corner of Fog Lane and Parrs Wood Road was a field called Kirk Oak, which lay on the north side of the lane. This too belonged to William Egerton. Kirk Oak went as far as the spot where Parrs Wood Road Congregational Church now stands. Having reached this spot our traveller was now at the boundary of the township, although some of the strips in Barcicroft, which lay nearby, and to which reference has already been made, were detached parts of Didsbury. Several of the strips in Barcicroft had long since been merged together into a field called Mr. Leadsome's Field, by which name it was known when our traveller would have seen it. The only possible explanation of this name is that it was farmed by Peter Leadsome, who was minister of Didsbury from 1650 to 1661. It may, indeed, have been part of the glebe. There was also a large detached part of Didsbury, known as the Dob Heys, through which the railway track now runs between Mauldeth Road and Burnage Stations. Near the Kirk Oak was a gate leading into Barcicroft.

On the opposite side of Fog Lane, at the township boundary, which is now marked by the junction of The Drive and Fog Lane, was a nicked oak which gave its name to Nicked Oak Field. Opposite Cow Lane were a few thatched cottages which were demolished in 1967. On the southern side of Fog Lane, also, were the Seven Intacks and Hughes's Tenement which have already been described.

The lane on the other side of the turnpike road, even then known as the Lapwing Lane, was of nothing approaching the same importance as Fog Lane. Passing along it our traveller would have Yannis's Twenty Acres on his left. A little past Yannis's Twenty Acres was a field the name of which was probably John Heppitt's Moorfields, although this is a little uncertain. This field stretched all the way to the road from Didsbury to Chorlton, which we now know as Barlow Moor Road. To the west again lay fields known as the Nearer Rough Moorfield and the Further Rough Moorfield, and afterwards as Birchfields. These took in the present sites of the Northern Lawn Tennis Club and Linden Road.

The tendency at the end of the eighteenth century was for small fields to be amalgamated into larger ones, but the converse seems to have been the case on the land where Old Lansdown Road and Clyde Road stand. Old Lansdown Road stands on land which had been known as the Little Moor Field, the Little Ley Field and the Paddock. Clyde Road stands on the site of the Great Moor Field, the Great Ley Field and the Lime Field. Previously, however, these six fields had formed one field called Lesser Moor Field or Long Nell Nook Field. The explanation probably lies in the fact that until the middle of the eighteenth century the whole district was part of Didsbury Moor. To the west of Lesser Moor Field were two long, narrow fields known as Silver John's Field and the Lower End of Silver John's Field. The former, which was part of Lum Farm, owned by Ann Broome, is now the site of Northen Grove. The latter, owned by Joseph Broome, a brother of William Broome of the Pump House, is the site of Cresswell Grove.

Walking to the end of the Lapwing Lane our traveller would have found that the lane he was on led into another lane which we now know as Burton Road, but which at that time had no name, being referred to merely as the lane leading to Red Banke, that being the field which lay where Darley Avenue joins Barlow Moor Road. On the east of the lane, that is to say on land now occupied by the Midland Hotel, West Didsbury Conservative Club and Albert Park Methodist Church, were fields known

78

as the Intake and the Six Acres. These were purchased by John Holt from Sir Edward Mosley in 1681. He was later made bankrupt and his lands sold to Adam Scholes and John Hudson. Eventually, in 1764, the holding was purchased by Samuel Egerton from whom they descended to the Egerton of Tatton family.

The road linking Hough End and Burton Road was in existence at the end of the seventeenth century. In the eighteenth century it was probably already known as Nell Lane, that name doubtlessly being derived from Long Nell Nook Field. It formed the boundary between Withington and Didsbury. Between that road and the road to Chorlton lay Barnfield, Barley Field, Beanfield, Turnip Field, Little Wheat Field, Great Wheat Field, Wellfield, Ffar Gin Field, Clover Field, Great Crowder Field, Great Garden and Little Garden, all owned by Ann Broome and farmed by Thomas Garnett. This area now accommodates Fielden Road, Barlow Moor Court, Newholme and the Government Buildings in Burton Road.

At the time our traveller passed along it School Lane was known as Warner's Lane. It began in the hamlet of Barlow Moor. What is now a busy cross-roads, controlled by traffic lights, was then known as Barlow Moor End. Much of the land at the commencement of Warner's Lane has been described elsewhere. On the north side stood the school of which we shall have more to say. When our traveller passed the schoolmaster was James Ward who was succeeded in that office in the early part of the nineteenth century by his son, James Walker Ward. As we have seen, James Ward lived in the house now known as Moor Cottage, Grange Lane, although the earlier schoolmasters probably lived in the school itself.

To the north of Warner's Lane also lay the Seven Intacks and Hughes's Tenement. To the south lay a large farm owned by Robert Bamford Hesketh and his son, Lloyd Bamford Hesketh, then both of Bamford, near Rochdale, but shortly to move to Gwrych Castle in North Wales. The farm, which stretched roughly to a line a little north of the present course of Ruabon Road, was made up of fields called the Black Croft, the Great Broad Field, the Little Broad Field, the Iron, the Piggott Carrs and the Meadow. The farmhouse stood where Ladysmith Road now ends. In a later period it became known as Whitehall Farm, but at the end of the eighteenth century it was called Burgess's in the Fields.

Warner's Lane was on the same site as School Lane, until a point a little to the west of the former television studios where it turned to the south. At this point was another small farmhouse which was known as Hulme's Tenement, not to be confused with Hughes's Tenement. The lane continued to the south until it reached the point where Parrs Wood Road now crosses the railway line. If our traveller walked along it there would have been fields called Nearer Crofter Field, Middle Crofter Field and Further Crofter Field on his left, occupying the site of the television studios and St. Mark's Secondary School. On his right would have been the fields of the Bamford Heskeths which we have just described. Behind him would have been a field called the Bowkhouse Field where now stands the Roman Catholic Church of St. Catherine of Siena.

At the point where Parrs Wood Road crosses the railway line the lane turned again, this time in the direction of Burnage. From that point onwards it still exists today in the form of a footpath which goes to the corner of Parrs Wood Lane and Burnage Lane. Walking along the footpath our traveller would be on the northern boundary of a group of fields called the Cockshut, the Clarke, Famous Pits and Bolton Wood Croft. These four fields were later made into one field called Famous Pits. Part, at least, of Famous Pits is now occupied by allotments which front onto Parrs Wood Lane.

An interesting explanation of the name of Famous Pits has been advanced by Fletcher Moss. At the spot which is now the corner of Burnage Lane and Parrs Wood Lane were a number of ponds, known as pits. The district may possibly have been that referred to several times in the parish register as the Pits. There is every reason to suppose that in December, 1745, part of the army of the Young Pretender passed this corner on their way to Cheadle Ford. Fletcher Moss has suggested that the pits may have become "famous" because of some unspecified incident which took place as they passed. While this explanation is purely conjectural there is no evidence to contradict it. Fletcher Moss, however, overlooked the fact that the Young Pretender was not the first prince whose troops passed that corner. In 1644 Prince Rupert led his army from Stockport to Barlow Moor on his way to relieve Lathom House. The incident which gave rise to the name may possibly have occurred on that earlier occasion, but Fletcher Moss's theory is rather supported by the fact that all the references to the Pits in the parish register are post-1644 and pre-1745.

If the traveller had decided to turn to the right at Barlow Moor End instead of to the left he would have found himself on the road to Chorlton, now known as Barlow Moor Road, but at that time as Barlow Moor Lane. At the corner was the Grey Horse Public House, which has long since been superceded by the Wellington Hotel. Our traveller would have found his journey along this road a lonely one. There may have been two or three cottages standing near the spot where Pine Road now joins Barlow Moor Road, and behind these there may have been three small fields called the Big Field, the Meadow and the Little Field. These cottages and fields were certainly there in the early part of the nineteenth century. There were also, probably, a few cottages where the shops now stand at the corner of Palatine Road and Barlow Moor Road. Apart from these our traveller would have seen very few houses fronting the road until he arrived at the spot where Princess Parkway crosses it. Here stood a farm. In the middle of the nineteenth century this was known as New Barns but when our traveller passed it does not seem to have had a name. For a number of years at the end of the eighteenth century it was the home of one Samuel Mycock, who farmed fields called the Little Moor Field and the Great Moor Field, the former being on the south side of the road, while the latter was apparently on the north side. They were owned by Ann Broome.

The fields on the north side of the lane have already been described. The names of those on the south side included, in almost every case, the words Moor Field. Hardy Moor Field had a long frontage to the road in the modern vicinity of Hesketh Avenue, Claremont Grove and Victoria Avenue. Lower Moorfield and Higher Moorfield stretched almost from the site of Lancaster Road to that of Mersey Road. Little Moor Field, as has been shown, was on the land through which Princess Parkway now passes. Ffar Moor Field and Nar Moor Field were opposite the site of Southern Cemetery. In addition to these the fields on which Bamford Road was built, which belonged to Robert Bamford Hesketh, were called Further Moorfield and Nearer Moorfield. Immediately to the south was Gaskill Moorfield, on the site of a few of the houses in Spath Road.

As well as the Moor Fields, a field called Little Sugar Field, behind which lay Great Sugar Field, lay where Lancaster Road joins Barlow Moor Road now. These were the property of Robert Feilden, as was Hardy Moor Field. They were tenanted by John Birch.

Standing a little off the main road, at the spot where Mersey Road and Spath Road now meet, stood a farm called Lum Farm. This fronted to the road for almost the whole distance between the points where Lancaster Road and Stanton Avenue now join it. It went as far south as the fish pond past which Palatine Road runs, and fronted the river between the loop at the northern end of Northenden Golf Course and the waste land now at the rear of Riverside Court. It comprised fields known as Lower Moorfield, Higher Moorfield, Beanfield, Swine Cotefield, Croft, Great Meadow, Croft and Orchard at Back o'th House, New Barn Field, Ffar Beanfield, Broom Nook, Old Marlfield, Bason Field, Sir John's Croft, Walker's Further End, Twyford's Further End, Wood's End, Well Field, Great Further End, Holme Great Hey, Little Hey, Horse Pasture, Old Meadow, Waste Land, Lum Cars, Red Bank Field, Pingot Bank, Har Moss and Waste Land. Silver John's Field which, as we have seen, is now the site of Northen Grove, was also part of the farm.

It is by no means easy to identify the locations of these fields and in many cases it is impossible. What is beyond doubt is that some of them were very small and were amalgamated early in the nineteenth century. Lower Moorfield, Great Meadow, Pingot Bank and Croft and Orchard at Back o'th House eventually became the site of The Beeches. Red Bank Field was immediately north of the loop in the river where Rowsley Avenue is now. There must have been at least one cottage in it since we find evidence that between 1672 and 1745 a family called Taylor had their home there. There is also reference to one John Burges living there in 1676. Holme Great Hey, Little Hey and Horse Pasture were in the vicinity of the fish pond and the site of Riverside Court.

In 1734 Lum Farm was owned by Rev. Dr. Francis Hooper, who was minister of Didsbury between 1721 and 1726, but he sold it at some time prior to 1746 to Richard Broome. At the end of the century it was owned by Ann Broome, who was Richard Broome's daughter. It appears to have been occupied at the end of the sixteenth century by a family called

81

Birch, although a family called Barlow lived there at the same time. There is also reference to one Thomas Wood living there between 1663 and 1691. Clearly there were cottages on the farm in addition to the main farmhouse. Between 1730 and 1741 references to a tenant called John Hulme are to be found. In 1783 John Rudd was the main occupier.

Also on the south side of the road and also belonging to Robert Feilden, and forming part of Samuel Mycock's holding, was Five Acres, which is now part of Christie Playing Fields and Nar Clover Croft and Far Clover Croft which were probably where Christ Church now stands. In the present vicinity of Derwent Avenue, Manor Drive and Macefin Avenue were Ffar Moor Field, Nar Moor Field, Ffurther Intake Meadow, Nar Intake, Croft and Rough Field. Fields called Nar Peas Croft, Peas Croft, Little Peas Croft, Croft and Orchard were in the present vicinity of Borrowdale Crescent and Craigmere Avenue. They were owned by John Bayley and Samuel Wright.

One field of the Barlow Hall estate was included in the township of Didsbury. On the Tithe Map of 1845 its name was given as Town Field, but that map was notoriously unreliable and the deeds of the estate do not show the names of the individual fields. It was bounded by the sites of Darley Avenue, Maitland Avenue and Merseybank Avenue.

A little further down the turnpike road from Grove Lane, then known as Crabb Lane, was a turning to the right at exactly the point where Dene Road now joins Wilmslow Road. This was Carr Brow Lane, or Car Lane, the name of which is now Ford Lane. This road still occupies its old position, although the commencement was lost in Dene Road, which is a modern creation. Near the point where Deneford Road and Ford Lane now meet was a narrow lane, which in the nineteenth century, led up to Ford Bank, the mansion house built by Joseph Birley in the early part of the nineteenth century. The early history of the Ford Bank estate, which included all the land now bounded by Ford Lane,, Lancaster Road and Spath Road is obscure, but it seems to have included fields called Sand Lands, Finney Townfield, Stock and Style Butts, Gaskill's Moorfield and Spaith Field, some, at least, of which were owned by the minister, Robert Twyford. There was also a small farm belonging to Robert Feilden, which lay in the vicinity of the junction of Lancaster Road and Dene Road. This was made up of Yannis Field or Far End, Walker's or Wood's New Field, Wood's Great New Field and Walker's Newfield.

Spaith Field has, of course, given its name to Spath Road. In 1780 it was the property of William Broome, who left it by his will to his son, John Broome. At that time it was tenanted by William Wood, who was the landlord of the Ring o' Bells.

Holt House and Highfield, with premises at the rear, stand on land which was known as Lady Bank Field, Orchard or Goose Croft, Nearer Turnip Field, Further Turnip Field and Shawcross Field or Croft.

Car Brow Lane ran into Stenner Lane, as Ford Lane does now, where the allotments lie. These allotments lie on land which our traveller would have seen as a field called the Bradley or the Braddiley. It belonged to

Robert Bamford Hesketh.

On or near the spot where Broomcroft Hall now stands there appears to have stood the home of Robert Twyford, who was minister of Didsbury from 1726 to 1746, and Mary Twyford, his wife. Since it is known that Rev. Twyford owned the land immediately to the south of Car Brow Lane, which now comprises a bank, on which stand magnificent tall trees, and land at the bottom forming the northern part of Simon Playing Fields, it can be assumed that he was a man of substance, a fact which would, no doubt, be reflected in the size and design of his house. The fields appurtenant to the house were called Car at the House, Broome Croft, Golden Bank, Pighew or Pighey, Carr, formerly Rushy Meadow and Thornhill's Car. The relative positions of these fields must remain a matter of conjecture, although in all probability Broome Croft was on the site of the house to which it gave its name. Car at the House was, no doubt, very near. Golden Bank was possibly the steep strip of land on which the trees stand. Thornhill's Car was undoubtedly the field immediately below the fish pond which, it will be recalled, our traveller saw on the turnpike road, immediately opposite the Pump House. The Pighew was adjacent to Golden Bank and was probably the land immediately to the south of it. In 1730 one John Hardy had his cottage there.

At the western extremity of the steep strip of land, near the Bradley, was a very small piece of land which bore the misleading name of Twenty Acres. This belonged to Robert Bamford Hesketh.

Stenner Lane is known to have borne that name at the end of the eighteenth century, although, curiously enough, it was not once described as such in the parish register. Although, as the road to Northenden, it must have been one of the major roads leading out of Didsbury, there is no reason to suppose that it was wider than it is today. Horse drawn waggons must have had the same difficulty in passing each other as motor vehicles have today.

At the end of the lane, adjoining Duke's Hill, were the chapel and the Ash House which have already been described. Fronting the lane between what are now the Old Parsonage and Stenner Brow were five cottages. In "Fifty Years Public Work in Didsbury" Fletcher Moss, who eventually became the owner of these cottages, gave a detailed history of them by reference to their title deeds. These deeds, it may here be mentioned, eventually came into the possession of Lord Ashton of Hyde, the owner of Ford Bank, by whom they were deposited at the Lancashire County Record Office, at Preston, where they can now be seen.

They show that at the end of the seventeenth century a messuage or tenement with two acres of land was sold by Sir Edward Mosley to Edward Hulme, a shoemaker. Only one house was referred to, that presumably standing on the site of Stenner Brow. Subsequently the holding became the property of Thomas Gaskell, who lived there. In 1775 Thomas Gaskell mortgaged it for £100 to William Wood who was described as a yeoman, but who was, in all probability, the same person as the William Wood who was the parish clerk and the landlord of the Ring o' Bells.

It is known that, at the end of the eighteenth century, there was a spot in Didsbury known as Gaskell's Brow, doubtless a steep road. While we have no evidence as to where it was it seems that it may have been that part of Stenner Lane immediately outside the farm which then stood on the site of Stenner Brow, taking its name from Thomas Gaskell. Here can be little doubt also that this was the spot referred to in the parish register, in 1713, as Didsbury Browe.

Further down the lane, on the right, were three cottages which still exist as Nos. 18 and 20 Stenner Lane, No 18 being composed of two cottages which have been joined together. These are rather older than No. 20. In the internal wall of No. 18 there can still be seen signs of a window which was bricked up when No. 20 was added on.

There would almost certainly be cottages on the south side of Stenner Lane, adjoining the church, but we have no record of their appearance. The land immediately at the base of the churchyard wall was known, appropriately enough, as the Ffield below the Church. Owned by John Bayley and Samuel Wright it was occupied by Mrs. Blomiley a widow.

To the north of the lane was a field known as Withy Ley, on the site of Simon Playing Fields, where, for many years, the Didsbury and South Manchester Agricultural Society held its annual show. This can almost certainly be identified with the land described in the Survey of 1322, as le Wetheheye. At the time our traveller passed it was farmed by William Wood of the Ring o' Bells. In Tudor times Withy Ley, at that time known as Whitley, was part of the lands of the Didsbury Chantry, as were the Great Birches, which were near Boathouse Farm. During the reign of Edward VI the chantry was dissolved and its lands seized by the Crown. Towards the end of the sixteenth century the Crown granted a lease of these fields to one William Ashurste for eight years, but possession was taken of Withy Ley by Ralph Twyford and the Great Birches by John Pickering. In 1582 the Attorney General of the Duchy of Lancaster, at the behest of William Ashurste, commenced proceedings in the Chancery Court of the Duchy to eject the intruders, but the result of the case is not known.

Opposite Withy Ley, on what are now football fields, were fields known as Croft, Car, Bush Meadow, Stenner and Acre. These also belonged to John Bayley and Samuel Wright. In 1783 they were tenanted by William Axon.

Our traveller has now reached the point where Stenner Lane and Car Brow Lane met. This district was known as Lane End. Here he would have reached the artificial banks which lined the river. Each section of the banks appears to have had a name. The section near Lane End was known as Alder's Fender. Near the present Stenner Farm was Owlers Fender, named after the Owlers, a field owned by the Bamford Heskeths, and now forming part of the football fields. Somewhere in the vicinity was Abigail

84

Wood's Fender. Abigail Wood was the owner of Shalcross Croft where the Limes now stand. Even in the eighteenth century the low lying land near the river was in constant danger of flooding, and our traveller may have seen workmen repairing the banks as he passed.

Mounting the river bank our traveller would have found himself looking at the river. The pathway he ascended still exists. In those days it led right down to the water's edge, being the approach to Northenden Ford. This descending path was visible until the early part of 1967 when it was levelled out.

It is not known when Northenden Ford came into existence. The earliest reference to it appears to have been contained in the letter written by Sir Wm. Brereton, quoted elsewhere in these pages, in which he discussed the many places where the river could be crossed. The ford crossed the river diagonally, the southern end being in exactly the same spot as the southern end of the present Simon's Bridge.

Let us suppose our traveller continued his journey on the southern bank of the river. Going down the lane, known as King's Lane, which now leads to Didsbury Golf Club, he would pass through an agglomeration of small fields which belonged, in the main, to Robert Bamford Hesketh although one of them, at least, is known to have been the property of Lawrence Walker, a Stockport attorney. It seems that in this area the land was still cultivated in doles. Some of the doles were known as Brown and Woods Doles and the Long Dole and the Broad Dole, which were also known as the Long Warth Dole and the Broad Warth Dole or the Long Northenden Warth Dole and the Broad Northenden Warth Dole. These lay at the northern end of King's Lane immediately adjacent to the river.

The field on which the Club-house now stands was known as the Warth Field or Hudson's Warth Field. It stretched as far behind the present building as the river. To the south of the present building, also fronting on the river, lay Twyford's Warth Field. In 1785 these fields were occupied by John Warburton and James Blomiley.

Opposite the Club-house, on what is now its car park, was Twyford's Warth Meadow, the property of the minister and churchwardens, purchased in 1775 for £200, provided as to half by Lady Ann Bland and as to half under the will of Thomas Linney, it became known as the Poor's Field. More of it is written elsewhere.

After passing Twyford's Warth Meadow King's Lane turned sharply to the left. Proceeding along it our traveller would have a field called King's Field on his right. After a few yards the road turned to the right. Proceeding further along it he would still have King's Field on his right. On his left was a field belonging to the Tatton family of Wythenshawe, that being all that remained to them of their once sizeable estate in Didsbury. They were, of course, also the owners of large estates in Northenden and Wythenshawe. Along the south west side of this field ran a brook. This formed the boundary between Didsbury and Northenden. It passed under King's Lane by means of a culvert.

Millgate Lane was known as the Millgate, Milnegate or Mylnegate, the name being derived from the fact that it led to the water mill on the banks of the Mersey. At the turn of the eighteenth century the home of Rev. John Newton stood at the corner of the lane and the turnpike road. At the other corner, where Millgate Square now stands, were premises owned or occupied by Thomas Whitelegg. Being the road to Gatley the lane would have been fairly busy. As we have seen, it was the route taken by a patrol of the army of the Young Pretender in 1745. On the right of the lane, going south, was the farm of William Wood, the parish clerk. The fields fronting to it were the Nar Shawcross Carr and the Far Shawcross Carr. On the opposite side of the lane was more land belonging to Robert Bamford Hesketh. Our traveller would have seen the row of old cottages which still stand facing Fletcher Moss Park.

At the point where it now joins Kingston Road the lane turned sharply to the right. Here it is now called Parrs Wood Road. On the left is an estate of houses comprising Maywood Avenue and Highbank Drive. Very little is known of the history of this land except that in a later day and age the fields were known as the Barn Field , the Middle Field and the Short Acre. It is quite likely that they were known by these names in the eighteenth century. Near the present junction of Millgate Lane and Parrs Wood Road was a farm-house. In 1821 the farm was owned by a family called Cookson, who owned it until 1913. They may have been the owners when our traveller passed.

It is very difficult to give a coherent description of the farms in the vicinity of which our traveller now finds himself, first because although we know the names of most of the fields any information as to their location has been lost for all time, secondly because many of the fields bore the same names, and thirdly because the farms were made up of several detached parts. Typical of such farms was that belonging to James Bayley and Samuel Wright and occupied, in 1783, by James Higgenbotham. This comprised Jones Hey, where Riverton Road now meets Broad Oak Lane, Tipping Field, facing Broad Oak Lane near its present junction with Tanfield Road, Yannis's Acre where Tanfield Road and Riverton Road meet, Gatley Fford Meadow, or Sandfield or Gatley Warth, where Millgate Lane, in that vicinity no more than a footpath, meets the river and Ffarther Wash, Great Wash, Wash, Slack, Long Rick, New Car, Side Car with Orchard, Car with Lane and Orchard and Car all of which were on the north side of Millgate Lane where the refuse tip is now. In addition to these fields there were Pall Croft, Ffurther Mun Field, Nar Mun Field, Barker Meadow and Gillmajor, the sites of which cannot now be determined.

The road now known as Broad Oak Lane led to a farm which was known as Broad Oak Farm. It was owned by Ann Broome. It was known by the same name as early as 1570, when it was in the occupation of Thomas Rudd, remaining in the occupation of his family for some 300 years. The farm house was in the approximate position of the present Broad Oak Cottage. As we have seen, the fields attached to the farm included Moor Bank, Moor Bank Meadow and the Patch which were on the football fields near Cheadle Bridge, and also Coppice Warth on the south bank of the river, but they also included Great Meadow, Vick Acre, Nar Wheat Field and Ffarther Wheat Field, Kiln Meadow, Ffox Field, Clay Field, Little Meadow, Kitchen Field, Barn Field, Nar Boat Field, Ffurther Boat Field, Croft and Orchard. The fields called Nar Boat Field and Ffurther Boat Field were adjacent to the river in the vicinity of Fairlands Drive. Their names suggest that there was a ferry in the vicinity.

Adjoining the river, and forming the modern site of Bankside Road and Narview Drive, was a field belonging to the Bamford Hesketh family known as Hen Ridings.

There was a farm house where Underbank Farm used to stand. It too was owned by John Bayley and Samuel Wright. Near it were fields called Basing Field, Car, Slack and Long Hey, which were on the site of Tuscan Road, Hudson's Hey, just south of Millgate Farm, Gatley Ford Field, which was on the approaches to (but not adjacent to) Gatley Ford, Long Rick and Beet Meadow on the refuse tip and Barn Croft, the position of which is unknown. They were tenanted by a Mrs. Kelsall.

Nearer to the river were fields called Croft, Acre, Midup, Nar Low Meadow, Ffar Low Meadow, Mill Hey and Car which were tenanted by John Hampson. The names of these fields reveal the position of the thirteenth century water mill, built by Simon de Gousil. In 1810 a second mill was erected on an island in the Mersey opposite Broad Oak Farm. The arm of the river, which was utilised as the mill race, was later filled in, thus joining the arm to Didsbury. In 1783 the island was occupied by John Rudd of Boathouse Farm.

Not a great deal is known of the history of Millgate Farm, which stands at the end of the lane, but it would seem to have been the property belonging to John Clarke which was offered for auction at the Ring o' Bells on 19th June, 1788, and described as follows:-

> "All that Messuage and Tenement with the outbuildings and about 12 acres 2 quarters and 4 perches of good Meadow and Pasture Land of Lancashire Measure thereunto belonging situate and being in Didsbury aforesaid now in the occupation of Samuel Heskey as tenant thereof.
>
> The Estate is free from payment of any Chief or quit Rent and Tithe Hay. The Buildings are mostly new and in good repair and the Lands are in good condition a Part whereof adjoins the River Mersey."

Unfortunately the names of the fields in Millgate Farm are not known but it would seem that the one adjoining the river was known as Mason's Meadow.

To the north of Millgate Farm was the Bench Croft. At the turn of the century it was the property of Thomas Hardern and was occupied by Samuel Hesketh (or Heskey) of Millgate Farm, but in 1817 it was sold to Robert Feilden. It had formerly been the property of Rev. William Twyford.

North of Bench Croft, and lying adjacent to the river was Kemp Patch. Owned by Robert Feilden, and occupied, in 1783, by John Hampson, this

87

was an outlying field attached to the farm which lay, in the main, where Didsbury Cricket Ground and Parrs Wood Railway Station are now.

In this district, north of the lane, most of the fields belonged to John Bayley and Samuel Wright, but there were a few, known as Long Ridges, which were owned by Robert Bamford Hesketh. They are now part of the refuse tip.

The Millgate took a winding course over what is now the football ground of the Old Bedians, until it reached the Mersey. At the meeting point of the lane and the river was a crossing place called Gatley Ford. It was at this spot that the Scottish patrol crossed the river in 1745. On the other side of the river the road took the name of Watery Lane, presumably because of the fact that Gatley Brook flowed alongside it. Here was one of the four parts of Didsbury, known as Gatley Carrs, or Gatley Eye, which lay on the south side of the river.

Gatley Eye can be approached from Longley Lane, Northenden. The southerly part, which is used as a refuse tip, is divided from the northerly part, which is part of Didsbury Golf Course, by railway tracks, under one of which is an arch, made to allow Watery Lane to pass. Nothing is known of the history of this part of Didsbury, except that it included the fields known as Broomfield, the Car Meadow and Watery Field, which, on 30th December, 1685, were given as the endowment of the village school by Sir Edward Mosley to John Rudd and James Blomiley, alias Bankes, the first trustees.

Near Parrs Wood the turnpike road met the road to Stockport. The land on the south side of the road to Stockport, now known as Parrs Wood Lane, was the Parrs Wood estate. On the north side were Greengate, where there is now an ominbus depot, and Famous Pits, through the site of which Kingsway runs.

As he turned up Burnage Lane the only building our traveller would have seen was the farmhouse where No. 1002 Burnage Lane now stands. For centuries this was known as Bolton Wood Gate, being so described in the parish register as early as 1597, when it was the home of Nicholas Holt. Attached to the farmhouse were fields divided into two quite separate blocks. The first block occupied the present site of Bolton Avenue, Lynwood Road and the lower end of Saddlewood Avenue, while the second block comprised Queensway, Riva Road, Albury Drive, the eastern extremity of the modern School Lane and the upper part of Saddlewood Avenue. Dividing the two blocks was a long, narrow field, which is now the site of Kinburn Road and the centre part of Saddlewood Avenue. This was known as Burnage Meadow and was the property of William Broome J.P. who inherited it from his father, William Broome. In the centre of Burnage Meadow was a pond which was eventually filled in to make way for Kingsway.

It would seem that in 1707 Bolton Wood Gate and the farm attached to it were purchased by Edward Hampson from William Brookes and William Brookes, his son. His family has lived on the site ever since. The present owner of the house, Mr. William Mitchell, is a descendant of the same.

family. In short the site has belonged to the same family for 260 years, a longer period, by far, than any other family in the area can show ownership of a piece of land.

To the north of the farm was another long, narrow field where Hurtsford Avenue now stands, but this was in the township of Burnage. To the north again, occupying land which now comprises Shortland Crescent and stretches westward to include Baldock Road and even part of Willow Way and Atwood Road, were four fields called the Nearer Town Field, the Further Town Field, the Crooked Acre and Hampson's Meadow. These were also the property of William Broome J.P. and at the end of the century were occupied by Ralph Pott. At some time in the early part of the nineteenth century they also were acquired by the Hampson family, thus becoming part of Bolton Wood Gate Farm.

Before 1862, when Palatine Road was opened up, the area now occupied by Withington Golf Course and the land lying between Marie Louise Gardens and the river, was a most inaccessible part of Didsbury and for that reason was not used for growing crops. It was divided up into quite large fields which were used exclusively for grazing livestock. Most of the fields were detached parts of farms lying elsewhere in the township.

The only way by which the area could be approached from Didsbury was by means of footpaths which still exist today. One of these commences near the northern end of Simon's Bridge and continues in a south-westerly direction across the golf course, passing the club house, until it reaches the river opposite the Tatton Arms Hotel. This was, in all probablity, the right of way which, as we have seen, Ralph Longford granted to Robert Tatton in 1539. The other branches off the first and runs in a north-westerly direction across the golf course to Palatine Road. In those days it continued as far as the footpath which still exists along the banks of the river.

Taking the first footpath, which in its easterly parts lay close to the river, our traveller would have passed through the Great Sandileys, which was owned by Robert Bamford Hesketh and was by far the largest field in the township. Adjacent to it lay the Little Sandileys. A little way down the path, on his right, the traveller would have found Burnt Ash, and on his left Ford Mouth, both of which are also owned by Robert Bamford Hesketh.

Further down still he would have come to the field on which Withington Golf Club House stands. This was known as the Hurstfield. At the time of his journey it was owned by Thomas and Mary Hardern, who purchased it from the minister, Rev. William Twyford. Previous to that we find that part of it was owned by the Rev. Robert Twyford, and occupied in 1733, by Harry Bancroft, while another part was owned by William Broome and occupied by Samuel Walker, the tanner, who was at that time the owner of the Pump House.

On his right, as he approached the river the traveller would have found the footpath skirting Northenden Boat Meadow, which was owned by Robert Feilden and tenanted, in 1783, by John Hampson, whose farm, it

89

will be recalled, lay on the sites of Didsbury Cricket Ground and Parrs Wood Railway Station. As its name suggested it included the landing place of the ferry boat which plied to and fro between Didsbury and Northenden. It is today a football ground owned by Wilson's Brewery Ltd.

Lying adjacent to Northenden Boat Meadow, in the position now lying between the football ground and Palatine Road, was Weir End. This was owned by Miss Ann Broome and was part of the farm, now forming part of Southern Cemetery, occupied by Benjamin Jackson. The name Weir End was a misnomer. The ancient weir ended in Northenden Boat Meadow.

The field, adjacent to the river, through the site of which Palatine Road now runs was Great Hey. Adjoining it on the east was Garnett's Rough. These also were owned by Ann Broome and occupied by Thomas Garnett, from whom, perhaps, Garnett's Rough derived its name. They were detached parts of a larger farm, this time the farm in the township of Withington which comprised a great deal of the present Southern Cemetery.

A little to the east of Palatine Road, lying between the present site of that road and the club house, was Yannis Meadow, or Dry Hey. This was owned by Robert Feilden and tenanted by Samuel Mycock. As we have seen Samuel Mycock lived on the site of the roundabout at the corner of Barlow Moor Road and Princess Parkway and had other fields in that vicinity.

If, instead of following the footpath to Northenden Boat, our traveller had branched off onto the other he would have found himself crossing the Great Sandileys and would have passed by an oak tree which even at that time was more than 350 years old.

Leaving the Great Sandileys the path continued through a field which was called Dockey Hey, but which had previously been known as Yannis's Rye Hey. This was the property of William Broome and was part of a holding known as Yannis's Tenement. Where the other parts of this tenement were located is not known. They were certainly not adjacent to Dockey Hey, which was bounded on the north, east and south by land belonging to the Bamford Hesketh and Feilden families, and on the west by the river. In short, like its neighbours, the field was a detached part of a larger holding. On 28th January, 1801, it was sold by William Broome to John Rudd of Didsbury, described as a yeoman. John Rudd's descendants still live on the site at No. 244 Palatine Road. At the time of the sale it was in the occupation of Joseph Goodier.

To the north of the Great Sandileys and Dockey Hey was a stream which can still be seen flowing across the golf course and passing under Palatine Road in a culvert. On the other side of the stream lay the Green Hey which is now the site of Nos. 230 to 242 Palatine Road, and Ash Field on the other side of the road. It was the property of Robert Bamford Hesketh. Also his property were the Little Crimbows, the Middle Crimbows and the Great Crimbows which took up the modern

90

sites of Heyscroft, the Government building at the corner of Dene Road West and the southerly half of Marie Louise Gardens.

To the north of the Green Hey, occupying the site now at the rear of Riverside Court, was a field which was referred to in various documents as Ogre, Ogrey, Ogree, Agrey and Auguries. At the time our traveller passed it was the property of Robert Bamford Hesketh, although at some time prior to 1814 it became the property of Wilbraham Egerton, the lord of the manor, since in that year we find him granting it to Robert Feilden in exchange for the Little Pea Field, the Far Pea Field and the New Field, which lay near where Christ Church is now, between Ambrose Drive and the river.

The Ogrey was the subject matter of a dispute which must have rocked the township. On his appointment to the living at Didsbury in 1720 Rev. Thomas Wright drew the attention of the lord of the manor, Lady Ann Bland, to an allegation that her ancestor, Sir Edward Mosley, had given the field to the Church. Lady Ann's reaction to these overtures may be judged from a letter which Rev. Wright wrote to the Bishop of Chester on 18th August, 1720.

> "Upon my last return from Chester Mr. Shrigley advised me not to enter on Didsbury till my Lady Bland's passion was a little abated, whereupon I omitted for three Sundays".

On being told that Lady Ann bore him no ill will but still asserted her right to the land, he showed his licence and officiated although he still complained of the treatment meted out to him by William Broome, the steward, and "six or seven vile, carnal, drunken wretches" by whom he was "persecuted and hunted like a partridge upon a mountain".

Rev. Wright ceased his ministry at Didsbury at the beginning of 1721, although whether he resigned or was dismissed is not clear. After his departure the question seems to have sunk again into the oblivion from which he lifted it. No further evidence has come to light since as to whether Sir Edward Mosley did or did not give the Ogrey to the Church. The next we know of it was in 1746, when it belonged to John Davenport of Stockport from whom the Bamford Heskeths inherited their estates.

The only part of the township which our traveller has not now visited is the northern tip of Northenden Golf Course, south of the river, opposite Darley Avenue. This was so isolated from both Northenden and Didsbury that there appears always to have been doubt which township it belonged to. It was known as Hoo Mow Meadow and, in 1820, it was part of Lum Farm.

Chapter VIII

VILLAGE LIFE IN GEORGIAN TIMES

Until the latter part of the nineteenth century the basic unit of local government, the legal pivot around which village life revolved, was the township or vill. From about 1663 onwards we find countless references to Didsbury, Burnage, Withington and Chorlton each being a township in its own right, but before that date the Manor of Withington, except such parts as lay in the Parish of Bolton, was one great, undivided township. This fact is evidenced by a variety of documents. For instance a commission appointed shortly after the execution of Charles I, to enquire into the number and value of church livings in Lancashire reported:-

"........... in the townshippe of Withington there are four Chappells;
    vidzt: Diddesbury, Birch, Chorlton and Denton".

The township of Didsbury seems to have owed its creation to the Poor Relief Act, 1662, which provided that in the sparcely populated counties of northern England the operation of the Poor Law was to be transferred from the parishes, which in that part of the country were very large, to the much smaller townships. The act seems to have been interpreted, on rather dubious authority, as authorising the sub-division of larger existing townships into smaller ones. Thus it was that the township of Withington was divided into nine smaller townships, Withington, Didsbury, Burnage, Chorlton, Rusholme, Moss Side, Levenshulme, Denton and Haughton.

As a general rule there is little or no mystery as to how the boundaries of these new townships were defined. Natural contours like the Ball Brook and the Cringle Brook were used as well as artificial ones like the Mickle Ditch and the fencing of Withington Demesne. In the case of the boundary between Withington and Didsbury it was drawn, for much of its length, along the roads which we now know as Nell Lane, Burton Road and Lapwing Lane.

Yet in some parts the boundaries were ludicrous. The townships did not even consist of continuous areas. There were many cases where detached parts of one township lay embedded in another. For instance, a large piece of land near what is now the junction of Hardy Lane and Darley Avenue was part of Withington, as was the land now occupied by Burnage Cricket Ground on the east side of Kingsway. A piece of land at the present junction of Green End Road and Kingsway was part of Didsbury. Lathom Road, Shireoak Road and St. Chad's Road stand on land which was a detached part of Burnage. A tongue of Withington stretched along what is now Palatine Road as far as its junction with Barlow Moor Road. In the words of one commentator the boundaries were "as jagged as a broken saw, and detached fragments are scattered about as if a bombshell had burst just there". The reason for this state of affairs was probably that the boundaries were drawn along the boundaries of existing farms. Hence the detached parts of the townships signified nothing more than that farmers cultivated holdings which lay in several detached portions. Such holdings are not uncommon in rural areas today.

In view of the fact that Didsbury and Withington owe their very existence to the Poor Law it seems not inappropriate, in considering the officials of the township, to turn first to the overseers of the poor.

Very little is known of their doings either before or after the creation of the smaller townships, but just before the time the splitting up took place the overseers seem to have wantonly neglected their duties as we can see from an Order of the Lancashire Quarter Sessions.

"Att the last generall Quartr Sessions of the peace houlden at Manchestr ye 20th day July last past It was ordered that the Churchwardens and Overseers of the poore of Withington should forthwith all of them meet together and consider of theire poore within the said Towne and lay an Assessment for the reliefe of them in some Competent manner or otherwise the fine of Ten pounds to bee imposed and levied upon such of them as shall make default herein which said Overseers have neglected and refused to meet and lay an Assessmt for reliefe of the poore soe that the poore are in great want the psons who refuse to meet are

Thomas Lees	
Charles Shepley	
John Hampson	Overseers of the
Nicholas Houghe	poore of Withington"
ffrancis Wood	
Thomas Taylor	
Randle Warburton	

After the sub-division there appears to have been only one person holding the office in Didsbury at any given time, he being elected annually at a meeting of the vestry in the Ring o'Bells. The only person who can be identified as having filled the position was James Ward, the village schoolmaster, who was the overseer for several years at the beginning of the nineteenth century. A fascinating reference to him has come down to us in the form of an entry in the account books of the Ring o'Bells, made in 1807, which shows that Thomas Wood, the landlord, received £2.1.8d from him for meat, liquor and lodging "when Thos Chatterton was taken into custody and married Ann Tipping". This was probably a reference to what was known as a knobstick wedding. Unmarried mothers and their children were obvious burdens on the Poor Rate and it was not uncommon for the overseer to bring to bear whatever pressure he was able to compel the father to marry the woman he had seduced. In this case the village constable, at that time one John Birch, was called in by Mr. Ward to exert his influence as well.

Some of the functions now exercised by the Local Authority belonged to the churchwardens, of whom there were two. Fletcher Moss has recorded how, in the middle of the nineteenth century, they exercised jurisdiction over the water supply. They seem also to have had the duty of inspecting the public houses. One of them entered an item in his accounts in 1725 "When I went to ye towns-end alooking ye Alehouse". As we have seen, Town's End was the site of Philip Godlee Lodge. The ale house referred to must have been the predecessor of the Olde Cock.

The churchwardens were assisted in their duties by a clerk, appointed by the minister. For no less than 250 years, from some date prior to 1590 until 1839, this official was a member of the Wood family, some of whom were also landlords of the Ring o'Bells. For how long the clerks and the landlords came from the same family we do not know, but both functions were certainly shared by them during the Napoleonic Wars and a reference in the parish register to the death in 1645 of "Thomas Wood of Didsburie alehousekeep" suggests that the association was a long one. The clerk's duties seem to have included preparing accounts for the other officers of the township. Some of them also kept the parish registers, although there is definite evidence that, for lengthy periods, this duty was undertaken by the ministers, the schoolmasters, and various other persons whom we cannot now identify. It must not be thought that the clerks were men of education. They all possessed the ability to write, which in those days was by no means universal, but the following entries in the burials section of the parish register, in the handwriting of Thomas Wood, who held the office from 1681 to 1717, are demonstrative of his standard of literacy:-

> John Hughas of ladday baren
> Richard Tounley of Vithington the Alder
> Danel Vood of more Hand
> Astar the daughter of John Barlo of Chrol
> Margaret Bamford Widdo of fellafild
> Huge Smith of Laufuensom
> A smoul Infant of Thomas Harday of didarey
> Samuel the sonn of John Roode of Brodhok
> Mistris Sollingstone of Houm Hole
> Thomas Bourdman of Riusshoum
> John Gimney of Chrolton the youngker

Essential to the existence of a township were its constables. By definition a township was a place which had constables of its own. The

94

title attached to the office is apt to be confusing. One of the duties of the constables was to maintain law and order in the township, but there the similarity between them and their uniformed namesakes of today ends. It was not a full time occupation, nor yet a permanent one. There appear to have been two constables in office at any given time. Once a year, during the early part of November, a meeting of the villagers was held at the Ring o'Bells when one of the two retired and another was selected for recommendation to the Withington Court Leet, at which the appointment was more or less automatically confirmed and the new constable sworn in. No special qualifications were required as long as the candidate was an able bodied man. Service seems to have been compulsory, although if the person appointed did not wish to accept office it was open to him to appoint a substitute. Thus on 24th November, 1805, Thomas Wood made an entry in his note book:-

> "Agreed with John Birch to serve the Office of Constable for me, at One Guinea & a half to pay one guinea when swore, a half guinea at End."

The constables were not paid for their services although their expenses were refunded to them at the end of the year.

Although our knowledge of the constables of Didsbury is small a little is known about them and their doings during the Napoleonic Wars. In 1796 the retiring constable was Samuel Hesketh, the tenant of Millgate Farm. In 1806, as we have seen, John Birch acted as a substitute for Thomas Wood and in 1815, James Ward, the schoolmaster, served.

The constables were, of course, expected to patrol the village and generally to keep order. We find that year after year, on 5th November, they attended at the village green, which is now the car park in front of the Didsbury Hotel, engaged in "watching the bonfire to prevent mischief."

There was no counterpart of the police station and hence no cells where prisoners could be kept until their removal to the New Bailey Prison, which stood in Bridge Street, opposite Salford Railway Station. It appears to have been fairly standard practice, when an arrest had been made, for the constables to hold their man at the Ring o'Bells, where they entertained themselves (and their prisoner) with the hospitality of that establishment; hence the following entry in the account book:-

> 1796.
> Octo19. Daniel Blomiley & Joseph Goodier, Constables
> & 3 Assistants having Smith, Rowley & Serjeant
> in Custody all Night.
> 1 pint & 2 Quarts Beer   1. 3.⎤
> 27 glasses Rum & Wine &
>   Water   9. 0.⎟ 11. 9.
> Eating in the morning   1. 6.⎦

As can be imagined the incidence of crime under this system was high, and was not lessened by the total absence of street lighting. Consequently, in 1788, a public meeting was held in Withington to consider the various felonies, trespasses and misdemeanours which had lately been committed, the offenders having escaped punishment. It was unanimously decided to form a society for prosecuting offenders and a fund was inaugurated to pay rewards to any person who should apprehend or inform the committee of any person guilty of an offence. The rewards ranged from 10/6 in the case of stealing or damaging coals or implements of husbandry to £3.3.0. for burglary or highway robbery.

The constables were also responsible for summoning and supervising the militia, the part-time soldiers who found a twentieth century counterpart in the Home Guard. For this they were responsible to the constables of Manchester from whom they received their instructions.

On 23rd March, 1807, John Birch, who, it will be recalled, was serving as a substitute for Thomas Wood, called a meeting of ley (i.e. rate) payers at the Ring o'Bells to consider and advise about raising men for the militia without a ballot. This meeting was clearly called to discuss Didsbury's part in raising forces to resist Napoleon should he commence his threatened invasion. During the previous year an Act of Parliament had imposed a quota of men on each county to be subdivided between the various townships and parishes by the Lord Lieutenant. So it was that Didsbury was called upon to raise 21 men between the ages of 18 and 30. Primarily volunteers were to be called for, but the Act provided that if the quota could not be raised by this means then the number was to be made up by conscripts, selected by ballot. We do not know whether the meeting did, in fact, recruit the required number of volunteers.

In such records of the constables of Didsbury as have come down to us there are frequent references to a duty known as setting the Winchester Watch, which seems to have been exercised twice a year in March and August. While the nature of the task is far from certain it may refer to the duty imposed on the constables by the Statute of Winchester to inspect the parish armour twice in each year. This was by no means a sinecure. The degree to which civilians carried arms in former days can only cause amazement today. On the death of William Garnett of Didsbury, in 1707, he was found to be in possession of one breastplate, one silver-hilted sword, one brass-hilted sword, one gun and one case of pistols; not a bad collection for one who was the village schoolmaster!

Not the least of the constables' duties was that of seeing to it that the other officers of the township, the surveyors of the highway, the collectors and the assessors were duly nominated.

By virtue of an Act of Parliament, dating back to 1555, each township was responsible for the proper maintenance of the highways within its boundaries, a task delegated to officials known as surveyors of the highway. As in the case of the constables appointment to this office required no special qualifications. Each year on 22nd or 23rd September the constables called a meeting at the Ring o'Bells at which a panel of names was drawn up. This was then submitted to the Justices of the Peace at the local *Quarter Sessions, who appointed two of the listed persons. They then held office for twelve months, beginning in November. Records of their year of office were left by the surveyors appointed in September 1795. They were John Rudd, a farmer, whose family still live at No. 244 Palatine Road, on land purchased by their ancestor, and the ubiquitous Thomas Wood, who served the office of parish clerk at the same time, in addition to keeping the Ring o'Bells and cultivating a considerable farm. Their first act was to draw up a list of the roads for which they were responsible. These were the roads which we now know as Wilmslow Road, Parrs Wood Lane, Millgate Lane, Stenner Lane, Ford Lane, Barlow Moor Road and Fog Lane, totalling 6 miles 316 yards in length. The other roads were repaired, inasmuch as they were repaired at all, by the owners or occupiers of the land which fronted onto them.

In addition there were references in Wood's accounts to repairs done to Slate Lane, that presumably being the current name of Burnage Lane, which even today becomes known as Slade Lane at its northern end, and Garratt Lane, the location of which is quite unknown.

Garratt Lane seems to have given Rudd and Wood great trouble during their year of office, since they allowed it to fall into such a state of disrepair that the township was prosecuted. A meeting of the villagers was accordingly held on 23rd June, 1796, when it was decided to defend the indictment, but it seems that by the time the case was heard new surveyors had been appointed and their records were not preserved. Hence the result of the prosecution is not known. All that is known of the other work which Rudd and Wood undertook during the year is that they went to considerable trouble to keep Northenden Ford in a fit state for traffic to pass, and they also did repairs to the road on the steep hill in Stenner Lane just beyond the church, known in those days as Gaskell's Brow.

Labour was provided for the surveyors by legislation, passed in the reign of Elizabeth I, under which every able-bodied man in the township was obliged to put in six days work a year on the roads or provide a substitute. The surveyors themselves were not exempted from this obligation by virtue of their office. When the road to Wilmslow was made into a turnpike road, under an Act of Parliament in 1752, the County Magistrates apportioned the obligation so that each villager had to work three days on the turnpike road and three days on the other roads, or get a substitute to do so for him. Once again we turn to Thomas Wood's account books for an illustration:-

1794		
June 2, 3, 4½, 5½	To Team 3 days to Turnpike Road	3 days Turnpike
Sep 26, 27	To 1 man 1½ day to Lane opposite Door	
June 1	To 1 man 1 day to fill at Stenner Lane	3 days Bye-way
	To 1 man ½ day to level at the Carr Gate	

The collector of rates and taxes was also elected, although in this case the villagers seem to have exercised more discrimination than was the case with the other officers, doubtless because the post required somebody who could not only read and write, but could do arithmetic as well. Not unnaturally the services of James Ward, the schoolmaster, were again enrolled, he being chosen at a meeting in the Ring o'Bells on 29th June, 1796, and serving, as far as we can see, at least until 1810. As we have seen he also served as overseer of the poor during the same period. Apart from the local rates he also collected Property Tax and Income Tax. Each year he paid the parish clerk the amount incurred by the constables in expenses, who then passed the money on to the constables themselves.

Curiously enough the assessment of taxes was also carried out by officers nominated by the villagers. In their cases four names were put forward by a meeting held each January and submitted to the Commissioners of Taxes who selected two from them. For some reason it was by no means uncommon for the constables to be appointed as assessors also, and even when this was not done they seem to have had the power to remit part of the Window Tax. There were frequent entries in their accounts for "liquor at a Meeting to sign the certificates of Poor Persons excused from the Window Ley".

During the period which we are now considering life in Didsbury was incomparably different from what it is now. For the most part the inhabitants were born there, lived their lives there and were buried there. There was no public transport. The London coach rattled through the village every few days but did not stop there. Consequently a visit to Manchester could only be made by those who owned a horse and cart or were able to beg a lift in one. The alternative was a six mile walk and, be it remembered, a similar walk back. The poorer members of the community probably looked on the journey as an exciting event to be planned in advance and looked forward to, although we know that a few of them made the journey regularly to sell their goods in Manchester Market.

For the most part the people were engaged in agriculture, although not a few of them worked at hand looms installed in their own cottages. There were, of course, the alehousekeepers, blacksmiths, shoemakers, joiners and saddlers as well as general labourers and a few domestic servants. Skilled tradesmen were virtually unknown in the village although repeated references to watchmakers makes it appear that Didsbury was a local centre of the craft.

Almost the only persons of any appreciable education were the ministers, Robert Twyford from 1726 to 1746, William Twyford, his son, from 1746 to 1795, John Newton from 1795 to 1807 and John Gatliffe from 1807 to 1840. The Broome family, who owned almost all the village, were also persons of some attainment. One of them, at the least, was an attorney-at-law, although it is doubtful whether he actually lived in Didsbury. An entry made in his account books by Thomas Wood shows that on 10th January, 1806, he paid a Dr. Hulme his bill of £1.6.0. and another entry shows that on 5th August, 1807, he lent an umbrella to a Dr. Halliwell. In all probability qualified medical attention was unknown in the village until the end of the eighteenth century or the beginning of the nineteenth, which goes some way, at least, to explaining the shockingly high rate of infant mortality which no serious student of the parish registers can fail to observe. It is very doubtful whether the standard of education of the schoolmasters was high.

It is difficult for people living in an age when the cinema has given way to television to visualize life in a community where the outside world was a closed book. Even newspapers were almost unknown in Didsbury. The accounts of William Wood, Thomas Wood's father, show that in November, 1792, he commenced to take four copies of the St. James's Chronicle, which, being published in London, did not reach him until three or four days after publication. These four copies were subscribed for by Rev. Newton, the minister, William Broome the squire, James Broome his brother, and Thomas Wood the future parish clerk. Apart from them nobody in Didsbury took a newspaper. Presumably the absence of demand for the papers meant that the service caused William Wood more trouble than it was worth, for in his notebook he recorded that on 4th August, 1795, he gave notice to his supplier to stop the papers and received the last copies on 6th August, 1795, less than three years after he had received the first.

Once a year the village had its wakes. This centred round a rush cart ceremony of a kind which was quite common in the villages of Lancashire. Originally it took place on 25th July, St. James's Day, but when the calendar was put forward eleven days in 1752 it was held on 5th August. The reason why St. James's Day was chosen for the festival has become lost in antiquity, but in all probability it was simply because the weather was favourable at that time of the year. It is not known when the custom of holding the wakes began, but the fact that in two entries made in the parish register on 25th July, 1605, it was thought worth while to mention that that was St. James's Day suggests that it was established at that time since it was not the usual practice of those who kept the register to distinguish dates in that way. Nor is it known when it first became the practice to have a rush cart. The earliest reference to it that can be found is an entry in the churchwardens' accounts which shows that on 21st July, 1734, they donated one shilling towards the expense of providing it. In all probability the rush cart was introduced at about that time. Lavishly decorated with flowers and ribbons it started its journey in Withington early in the morning and was drawn in procession to the village green at Didsbury, accompanied by the entire population of the villages. It is said that the figures 1603 were embroidered in flowers on the side of the cart although the authority for this is very uncertain. If it is true no reason is known why that date should have been commemorated, but it is tempting to recall that it was the year in which James I ascended the throne. As we have seen, the local people were ardent supporters of the Stuarts during the Civil War and it may have been that the date on the cart was meant to commemorate the year in which that ill-fated family commenced to rule. The fact that the first Stuart king bore the same name as Didsbury's own saint was, in all probability, pure coincidence, for it is improbable that the villagers would choose to mark the commencement of his reign only two years after it began. The church was not formally dedicated to St. James until as late as 1855 when the identity of Didsbury with that saint made the choice of name an obvious one.

Quaint ceremonies and traditions grew around the rush cart and by the end of the eighteenth century the occasion saw the village green as the scene of general rejoicing. The holiday spirit lasted for several days during which the landlords of the inns were obliged to engage large numbers of extra staff.

There were a number of social clubs in the village, one of which was the Didsbury Hunt. Of the hunt itself we know very little, apart from the fact that on 28th January, 1793, it entertained the populace at the Ring o'Bells to witness the burning of an effigy of Thomas Paine, author of "The Rights of Man", then only recently published. It seems to have been linked very closely with another club, called the Didsbury Archers, which also met at the Ring o'Bells, the members amusing themselves by practising archery at shooting butts which lay where the tennis courts now are in Fletcher Moss Park. The archers seem to have held an annual dinner each September. Prominent in their affairs were Rev. Newton, William Broome and James Broome.

Much the same kind of club was the Gentlemen Bowlers, or to give it its proper title, the Gentlemen Members of the Bowling Green. This seems to have been inaugurated in 1794. In that year Rev. John Newton built a house on the land occupied by the shooting butts and the archery club seems to have gone out of existence. The bowling club was probably its successor, largely composed of the same members. They used the bowling green which still lies behind the Didsbury Hotel, a privilege for which they each paid the landlord 5/- per annum. They too held their annual dinner in September. It seems to have been a very exclusive club, for we know of it that in 1803 it had only ten members and the following year only eight.

If there were any similar clubs for men of the poorer classes no record of them has come down to us, although there seems to have been a fishing club which, no doubt, fished the Mersey. On the other hand there was a friendly society based at the Grey Horse, which stood on the site of the present Wellington Hotel and which appears to have been known also as the Ball and Nimrod. Thus it was that John Rudd, the same person as was overseer of the highway in 1794, and who died in 1810, left to his servant, John Taylor, the sum of £4.4.0. which was payable to his executors "from a Sick Society held at the Ball and Nimrod in Didsbury".

We know more about the Didsbury Female Friendly Society than of any of its contemporary organisations as a copy of its rules is still in existence. It was founded on 9th September, 1799, at the Ring o'Bells when two stewards were appointed and they, together with eleven other ladies, were constituted into a committee to draft rules. These rules were presented on 7th October, 1799, when it was agreed that the officers should be a president, two stewards, two wardens, two warders, a clerk or secretary and an assistant secretary, that the subscription should be 1/6 per quarter, that four shillings per week should be paid to sick members for the first twelve months and afterwards two shillings per week and that the funeral allowance was to be £5 to a member.

The society resolved to meet at the Ring o'Bells four times a year on the first Monday in each January, April, July and October. It is not known what took place at the meetings but the drinking of liquor was, from all accounts, an important part of the proceedings. The two wardens were responsible for seating the members and serving the liquor. The warders attended near the door to see that only members were admitted and to answer enquiries while the stewards collected the dues and visited sick members.

The rules laid down a scale of fines for various offences:-

"Any member not keeping silence during the club
hours when bidden by the president, or
behaving disorderly after being forbidden

	s.	d.
shall forfeit	0	2
The same for swearing	0	2
The same for entering intoxicated with liquor	0	2
Any member rehearsing a dispute after it has been settled shall forfeit six-pence	0	6
Any member striking another member during club hours shall forfeit five shillings and if they both proceed to fighting they shall forfeit five shillings each	5	0

Finally every member was enjoined to use her utmost endeavours, both by advice and example, to suppress and discourage vice, profaneness and immorality and promote virtue, industry, piety, honesty, decency and sobriety, to the Glory of God, her own welfare and the honour of her country.

It must not be thought that those who fell upon hard times were dependent solely on the Poor Law or the friendly societies. Didsbury was richly endowed with charities. Chief among these was Bland & Linney's Charity. During her lifetime Lady Ann Bland gave the sum of £100 to the churchwardens of Didsbury to be placed at interest and the income to be used for the benefit of poor housekeepers in Withington, Didsbury, Chorlton, Burnage and Heaton Norris. By his will dated 2nd June, 1763, Thomas Linney, a tailor of the Parish of St. Ann, Westminster, left a legacy of £100 to the churchwardens, the income of which was to be divided among such poor of the Parish of Didsbury as should not be under the common relief or arms of that parish and whom the minister and churchwardens deemed the most deserving. In point of fact there was not, at that time, a Parish of Didsbury. The parish church was the building which we now know as Manchester Cathedral, which served a parish stretching from the River Mersey to the northern boundary of Blackley, but the legacy seems to have been interpreted as referring to Didsbury as a township.

In 1775 the two gifts of £100 each were utilised by the churchwardens to purchase Twyford's Warth Meadow, that being the name of the field on the south bank of the river, later known as the Poor's Field, and remembered as such by people living today, which is now the car park of Didsbury Golf Club. This was let to a tenant. The resulting income was not distributed in cash but was used to purchase blankets, petticoats and stockings. Half of these were distributed to the poor of Didsbury each year so as to satisfy Thomas Linney's wishes. In accordance with Lady Bland's the other half was distributed to the poor of Withington, Didsbury, Chorlton, Burnage and Heaton Norris in rotation. Each family received one blanket, one petticoat, one pair of men's stockings and one pair of women's. The last such distribution took place in 1831.

Bland and Linney's Charity became linked with two other charities. The first was created by Sir Edward Mosley, Lady Bland's father, who, by his will, executed in 1695, charged the manors of Withington and Heaton Norris with the payment of a yearly sum of £4 to the churchwardens of Didsbury for the use of the poor of Withington and Heaton Norris and a yearly sum of £4 to be paid to the schoolmaster of Didsbury. By the beginning of the nineteenth century the trustees were paying the sum of £4 per annum to the churchwardens who lumped it together with half the rent of Twyford's Warth Meadow and distributed it in accordance with the terms of Lady Ann Bland's gift.

Secondly there was the Hampson Charity. By his will, made in 1756, Edward Hampson of Bolton Wood left the sum of £400 on rather complicated trusts which included annual payments of £1 to the preaching minister of Didsbury, £1 to the schoolmaster of Didsbury and £1 to the singers of Didsbury Chapel. Any residue was to be utilised as his executors should think fit. The executors, who were members of the Broome family, found it convenient to pay this residue, which amounted to about £2 per annum, to the churchwardens to be distributed with the other half of the rents of Twyford's Warth Meadow in accordance with the terms of Thomas Linney's Will. In addition the sacrament money collected in the church was distributed with the Linney and Hampson Charities, although part of it was handed to poor persons at the altar.

There were also the Boardman and Chorlton Charities. Sergeant Boardman, who lived on the spot now occupied by Didsbury Telephone Exchange, by his will made in 1768, left a legacy of £50 to provide funds to be given in bread in Didsbury Chapel on every Sunday to such of the most poor and indigent people living in and belonging to the several townships of Didsbury, Withington, Heaton Norris and Burnage, such as should come frequently to hear divine service at Didsbury Chapel as they in their discretion should think fit.

The Chorlton Charity cannot be better described than by quoting the entry in the Parish Register relating to its founder's burial:-

"13th January 1729
Thomas Chorlton de Grundey-Hill Heaton who left ffour pounds per Ann:

102

to Didsbury Church for ever to be given in bread by the Church-wardens each Sunday to such poor persons of the Townships of Heaton, Didsbury, Withington and Burnage as come to Divine Service. And twenty shillings per Annum to the School for ever payable out of ye land at Grundey-Hill."

Finally, in 1778, Miss Ann Bamford, one of the family from whom Bamford Road derives its name, left £100 "for the benefit of such poor housekeepers within Stockport, Cheadle Hulme and Didsbury not receiving relief from their Town" but all record of this legacy has been lost and it is not known what became of it.

Chapter IX

THE SCHOOLS

The origins of Didsbury's first school are shrouded in mystery and will ever remain so. That there was a school nearby, at Chorlton, in the early years of the seventeenth century we are quite certain, since it was mentioned in the will of Sir Nicholas Mosley, of Hough End, who died in 1612, but the first hint we have of a school in Didsbury is in the parish register, which recorded the baptism of "Mary daughter of Mr. Turner Schoolemaster" on 21st October, 1627. Later entries showed that the schoolmaster's full name was James Turner. He was buried in Didsbury Churchyard on 8th January 1669, being then still described as "Skoolmaster". Clearly he was only in the early part of his term of office in 1627. In 1641 he officiated at the funeral of one of the Royalist army, killed at the siege of Manchester and buried in Didsbury churchyard.

On the assumption that Mr. Turner's school was in Didsbury it is not known how it was financed, but by a will made a few days before his death in 1665 Sir Edward Mosley, at that time aged only 27, made the following provision:-

> "And I doe hereby give & bequth the several legacies hereinafter herein mentioned to be satisfied and paid with and out of the Rents issues and proffitts of my said Hereditaments (Except as aforesaid) and out of the said rest and residue of my said personal Estate (that is to Witt) the summe of foure score pounds to be laid out in the purchase of some lands Tenements or Rent for an Estate in Fee Simple and the proffitts thereof Yearly to be for the maintenance of a Schoole-master at Didsbury aforesaid for ever or towards the same".

The four score pounds do not appear to have been invested as directed by the will, and indeed there is nothing to suggest that any attempt was made to give effect to Sir Edward's wishes until 1685, at the end of which year his first cousin, also called Sir Edward Mosley, who had inherited his estates, granted to John Rudd, who was at that time the tenant of Broad Oak Farm, and Thomas Blomiley, alias Banks, both described as yeomen, land described as "All that and those the several closes and parcels of land commonly called and known by the name of the Broomfield, the Car Meadow, and the Water Field with their appurtenances situate lying and being on the South Side of the River Mersey reputed and taken to be within the Township of Didsbury in the Manor of Withington containing by estimation four acres of land or thereabouts be the same more or less". This piece of land is now occupied partly by the southernmost end of Didsbury Golf Course, partly by the Manchester Corporation Refuse Tip, approached from Longley Lane, Northenden, and partly by the railway line running from Northenden to Cheadle. It was known in the eighteenth century as the School Lands. Although the gift was expressed to be "for the performance of the last Will and Testament of the said Edward Mosley late of Houghend Hall" the deed whereby it was made went on to impose the condition "that he the said Schoolmaster be such as is approved of and comes in there by the consent and good likeing of the said Edward Mosley his heirs and assigns Lords of the Manor of Withington aforesaid". This condition did not, of course, have any justification under the terms of the will.

At some time the deed came into the possession of the chapel wardens of Didsbury and was eventually deposited by their successors at the Manchester Central Library, where it is open to inspection by the public. Although the will created an endowment for a schoolmaster, and the deed of 1685 made a gift of fields to secure an income, neither of them made any gift of a schoolhouse. Nevertheless, in course of time, a schoolhouse appeared in the road then known as Warner's Lane but now known (for obvious reasons) as School Lane. It stood on the north side of the road, near the present Didsbury Branch of the Manchester & Salford Trustee Savings Bank. It was demolished in 1878 to make way for the railway. When the building was erected, or how the land was acquired, it is impossible to say. If there were any title deeds they have long since been lost. There was a passing reference to the building in the will of Thomas Chorlton, made in 1728, but the only real record we now have is contained in a document dated 24th May, 1827, which recited:-

"Whereas there is an ancient schoolhouse in Didsbury aforesaid together with a plot of land adjoining attached thereto containing about one thousand square yards be the same more or less And whereas the said schoolhouse and plot of land have been uniformly occupied and enjoyed together by the schoolmaster of Didsbury aforesaid for the time being to whom the rents of the said hereditaments and premises——are applicable as well for the purposes of his own residence as for those of a school and are free from all rent except—a certain yearly chief or quit rent of three shillings which has been invariable paid by the said schoolmaster—"

The condition that the schoolmaster hold office at the pleasure of the lords of the manor had an interesting history. By 1827 we find that the schoolmaster of the time was nominated by Robert Feilden, who, as we shall see, was the major landowner of the district, although he was never the lord of the manor, that position being held at the time by Wilbraham Egerton of Tatton Park, Knutsford. How this power became exercised by Robert Feilden cannot be satisfactorily explained, but the explanation may have been connected with the chief rent of 3/- payable out of the schoolhouse. In 1752 we find the schoolmaster of the time, a Mr. Hudson, paying the chief rent to Sir John Bland, lord of the manor. As we have seen Sir John Bland's estates in Didsbury were eventually acquired by the Broome family. These estates evidently included the chief rent, for in 1783 that rent was inherited, with other property, by Frances Bayley from her father Richard Broome. Robert Feilden inherited the rent, with considerable other landed estates, in 1820 from Frances Bayley, who was his aunt.

Thus, although it was intended that the power of nominating the schoolmaster should belong to the lord of the manor, it seems to have been accepted, in course of time, that it was exercisable by the person to whom the chief rent was paid. If Wilbraham Egerton, to whom the right legally belonged, ever became aware of the irregularity he doubtless shrugged his shoulders and sank deeper into the luxuries of Tatton Park.

During the seventeenth and eighteenth centuries, the school received three supplementary endowments:-

First, Sir Edward Mosley of Hulme Hall, who was the same person as had given the fields to the school in execution of his forbear's will, himself left the schoolmaster an annuity of £4 by his own will, made in 1695, such annuity to be paid until land of the like value was settled. No such settlement was ever made and the annuity was charged on certain buildings and tenements in Didsbury. Where these were is not known, but in 1754 they were occupied by one John Shuttleworth. Also charged on them was a second annuity of £4, left by Sir Edward to the church wardens of Didsbury for the use of the poor of the manors of Withington and Heaton Norris.

Secondly, Thomas Chorlton, of Grundy Hill, Heaton Norris, whose death in January 1729 was recorded in the parish register, bequeathed an annuity of 20/- to the schoolmaster for the time being of the schoolhouse at Barlow Moor End, to be charged on his property at Grundy Hill.

Thirdly, Edward Hampson, an innkeeper of Withington, by his will, made in 1811, left the schoolmaster an annuity of 20/-.

In addition to the income received from these legacies the Didsbury School received payments from time to time from the Warden and Fellows of the Collegiate Church at Manchester. The nature of these payments is most obsecure. They were part of what was called "absence money" which one can only assume was money deducted from the stipend of the Warden or one of the Fellows of the College by reasons of his absence.

In 1767 absence money of two guineas was sent to Didsbury and utilised as follows:-

Josiah Downes	0. 1. 6.	
School wages for a son	0. 4. 6.	
of ——— Cash		
Do. for a son of ——— Holt	0. 4. 6.	
Do. for two sons of Thos Fletcher	0. 6. 0.	
Do. for Tho Fletcher	0. 3. 0.	
Do. for Wilm John Blomeleye	0. 12. 0.	
Do. for Jas. Hardeye	0. 4. 6.	
Six dozen of penny loaves		
distributed in the church upon		
3 Sundays to such poor people		
as frequent divine service	0. 6. 0.	
	———	
	2. 2. 0.	

No record of the schoolmasters has been kept and it is now impossible to compile a complete list.

James Turner we have already met. There is no evidence whatever that he was the first holder of the office, but if he was not we know nothing of his predecessors.

Rev. John Booker, who made a searching perusal of the Bishop of Chester's archives, recorded that in 1699 one William Garnett resigned the office of schoolmaster and submitted the name of Henry Smith to the bishop as his successor, the right of nomination having been delegated to him by the lord of the manor. Mr. Smith's burial, on 9th February, 1742, was recorded in the parish register, he being then described as "ye old Schoolmaster at Did". He actually retired in 1722 whereupon Thomas Hudson was appointed at the nomination of Lady Ann Bland.

Mr. Hudson was mentioned in the attendance roll of the Court Leet and Great Court Baron of Withington for the session of April 1734, as one of the inhabitants of Didsbury who attended, and we find him mentioned again in one of Sir John Bland's title deeds, dated in 1752, as the person from whom a chief rent of 3/- per annum was collected. It is too obvious to allow of doubt that this was the chief rent payable out of the school buildings.

In 1790 the parish register mentioned the baptism of "James Walker Ward, son of James Ward Schoolmaster of Didsbury". Further references to James Ward are to be found in the account books of the Woods, landlords of the Ring o' Bells, and also in the title deeds of Moor Cottage, Grange Lane, which was his home. The writer has been allowed to inspect these deeds by the kindly courtesy of Miss Joyce Owen the owner. In them James Ward was several times referred to as the schoolmaster. One of the deeds, dated 5th April, 1823, was manifestly executed after his death, but it referred to his son, James Walker Ward, the same person as was baptised in 1790, as being the schoolmaster also. Clearly he took over the position from his father. He died in 1837 a few days after his 47th birthday.

In 1836 we have the first reference to a schoolmistress in Pigot's Directory. Her name was Jane Taylor.

The identity of the schoolmaster in the middle part of the nineteenth century is a matter of some doubt. Pigot's Directory, 1847, gave his name as William Dukes, and Slater's Lancashire Directory, 1861, showed William Dukes as the master, and Elizabeth Dukes as the mistress. On the other hand the Lancashire Directory, 1858, mentioned Squire Heaton as master, Miss Annie Wilson Taylor as mistress and Miss Jane Lowry as infants mistress.

The educational facilities of the 'township at about this time were described in the Didsbury Church Hand-Bill for 1843:-

"The Schools

1. The Juvenile School is open for boys and girls above six years of age.

2. The Infant School is open for children under six years of age. In both schools the children are expected to be punctual, clean and tidy; and to bring their school pence each Monday morning, otherwise they will be turned back. Thus, we hope, the children, and their parents likewise will be trained to punctuality of payment, and to observe the Scriptural precept "Owe no man anything; but to love one another (Rom.xiii 8).

3. The Sunday School is opened at nine o'clock in the morning, and at a quarter before two in the afternoon. As the time for Sabbath school instruction is necessarily short, punctuality of attendance is especially enforced".

Between 1865 and 1871 the Lancashire Directory showed George Scott as master, Elizabeth Berry as mistress, and Jane Lowry as infants' mistress. In 1873 the mistress was Matilda Challinor. In 1879 the master was Samuel Brown, the mistress Mary Jane Walsh and the infants' mistress Mary A.Hampton. By 1881 the infants' mistress was Miss McCleary.

Consequent on the Report of the Charity Commissioners, in 1826, the legal standing of the school was drastically reorganised. The original trustees, John Rudd and Thomas Blomiley, alias Banks, were, of course, long since dead. An inspection of the parish register and the gravestones in the church yard revealed that Thomas Blomiley, alias Banks, had died on 1st December, 1695. John Rudd had survived him for many years, dying in January, 1723. It was ascertained that the legal ownership of the school was vested in his grandson, John Rudd. On the reorganisation John Rudd was allowed to remain as one of the trustees but he was prevailed upon to appoint Robert Feilden, Rev. Robert Mosley Feilden, his son, and one James Rudd to be trustees with him.

It was then provided that in the future the rents of the school land were to be used primarily for the repair and improvement of the school building, only the residue being used to pay the schoolmaster. On the occurrence of a vacancy the trustees, not the lord of the manor, were to appoint the new schoolmaster. The only children to receive instruction in the school were to be those actually living within the Chapelry of Didsbury, that is to say in the townships of Didsbury, Withington,

Burnage and Heaton Norris. The course of instruction to be pursued was to comprise a competent knowledge in the English language, writing and common arithmetic and finally all the children were to be educated by the schoolmaster in the religious principles of the Established Church of England, he being particularly required to attend to this part of their education as well as to their moral conduct. The trustees were given power to make further rules and regulations for the government of the school and in the event of disagreement among them the majority were to prevail.

In 1831 or 1832 the school came in receipt of financial support from the National Society of the Church of England and in 1842 an infant school room and a cottage were added to the older building, the cost being met by public subscription. In 1851 the school came under Government inspection and a Parliamentary grant was received. At that stage it assumed the name of the Didsbury Endowed National School.

The school lands on the south bank of the river were sold in 1863 to Mr. E. W. Watkin, the owner of Rose Hill, Longley Lane, for the sum of £871.2.6. which was invested in Consolidated Stock and in 1878 the school house was acquired by the Midland Railway Company, under its powers of compulsory purchase, and demolished. The compensation agreed on was £3,500, and this was used to build a new Church School in Elm Grove, where it still flourishes.

It is not known how many children the original little school was intended to accommodate, but in 1847 William Dukes was teaching only 40 children and receiving a salary of £50 per annum. When it is remembered that the population of Didsbury, at the time, was 1,248 it will be realised how grossly inadequate the facilities were by modern standards. It is not difficult either to imagine the difficulties of a lone schoolmaster teaching children of all ages and all standards in the same class!

The children who did not attend the day school helped their parents at the hand looms, or on the farms, or simply ran wild. For them the only vestige of education was at the Sunday school, which is known to have been in existence in 1803, when Thomas Wood noted that he had received 15/5 from Mr. Benjamin Brooks, churchwarden, for Sunday school books. He later became the parish clerk and it was probably to the Sunday school that Fletcher Moss was referring when he wrote of the clerk's house which stood in the front garden of the Old Parsonage and had been used as a school.

The deplorable lack of education in Didsbury was slightly ameliorated in 1863 with the opening of "The Didsbury Village School" on the initiative of Rev. Wm. Kidd.

Rev. Wm. Kidd had been appointed a trustee of the old school in 1851 but he was, apparently, soon at loggerheads with his co-trustees over the question of religious education there. Never noted for accepting defeat gracefully he did not resign as a trustee, but called a vestry meeting of pewholders of St. James's Church, which met in that church on 7th May,

1861.when the following resolution was carried unanimously:-

"That the following Gentlemen (with power to add to their number) be appointed a Committee, to consider the desirableness and practicability of erecting a suitable Building within the Parish of St. James for Educational and other purposes, in connection with the Parish Church.

The Rector and Churchwardens,
Mr. Hugh Birley and Mr. Moss."

The names of Messrs Dorrington and Sewall were afterwards added. The committee met six times, Rev. Kidd being appointed treasurer, and by the beginning of 1863 a small school had been erected, fronting to Wilmslow Road, on land which now forms the garden of No. 2, Kingston Road, at a cost of £600, raised largely by the efforts of the rector's wife. The estimated annual cost of the school was £40. This was exclusive of the cost of a singing class, the expense of which was defrayed from another fund.

Appealing in February to his parishioners for funds to carry on the school Rev. Kidd wrote:-

"As Rector of the residuary Parish of Didsbury, it is, as all will admit, my clear and bounden duty, to take care that the educational wants of the young children around us, and of the youths and adults, especially the farm labourers and other out-door servants and operatives who live in our midst shall not be lost sight of or neglected. To wean the youths and farm lads in our village from the temptations of the idle corner, the beerhouse, the tap-room, by winning them to desire self-improvement, and by helping them to learn and to love to read interesting and useful books especially the book of books—the Bible; and to promote such objects through evening classes and occasional Public Lectures. This surely is worth an effort, even in the southernmost and rural part of the Township of Didsbury."

The Didsbury Village School was demolished in the early part of the twentieth century. No vestige of the building now remains, but the most cursory inspection of the site will show that it must have been ludicruously small and totally unsuited for its purpose. A few of its former scholars still live in Didsbury today..

In the second half of the nineteenth century Didsbury saw the establishment of a plethora of small private schools. In 1847 Eliza Fletcher was the proprietor of a boarding school. Where it was carried on is not known. Her school was still in existence in 1861. In 1858 Miss Dorothy Hughes was the proprietor of a ladies' boarding school in Didsbury Park. Subsequently we find mention of schools under the Misses Booth in 1861, Charlotte C. Cunningham of Willow Bank, Palatine Road, in 1879, (this was a boarding school) and Helen McGowan of Grove Place, also in 1879. These all seem to have been "dames schools" which were carried on in the homes of their proprietors. It is hardly likely that the standard of tuition was high.

In the Lancashire Directory of 1865, 1869 and 1871 we find rather mysterious references to a second infants' school employing a single mistress. Where it was situated, or under whose auspices it was conducted, is not known. Whoever was responsible for it appears to have found difficulty in keeping the schoolmistress. In 1865 she was Catherine Deane, in 1869 Euphemia Willis and in 1871 Emily S. Scaddon.

At some time between 1825 and 1830 the small group of Methodists who were accustomed to hold services in the house of Elizabeth Johnson, which stood on a site between the present Warburton Street and School Lane, inaugurated a Sunday school of their own which is thought to have been held in a cottage very near to Mrs. Johnson's. This accommodation soon proved too small, and in or about the year 1830 the school was moved to the building formerly occupied by Messrs Mycocks, plumbers, at 754 Wilmslow Road, but then occupied by James Worsley, smith and wheelwright. A room on the upper floor was rented at £4 a year and used not only as a schoolroom but as a place of worship as well. The Sunday school sat from 9 a.m. to 11 a.m. after which an address was given. There was a further session of the school in the afternoon followed by a service.

By 1839 the room above the wheelwright's shop was no longer large enough to accommodate the growing congregation and a new building was specially erected by one of the group, James Worsley, in Whitechapel Street, then known as Chapel Street. This consisted of three cottages on the ground floor above which was one large room which the congregation rented at £9 a year. Like its predecessor this room was used as both a place of worship and a school, and was given the name "Barlow Moor Wesleyan Chapel and School".

The teachers at the Sunday school were employed on a part time basis. The earliest records, dated in 1851, show that in that year there were no less than nineteen teachers for only eighty-four pupils.

The school in Chapel Street was, of course, a Sunday school only. Weekday education could only be had by the Methodist children at the Didsbury Endowed National School where, it will be recalled, the religious principles of the Church of England had to be taught. This state of affairs was satisfactory to neither party. For the methodists the drawbacks were obvious and Rev. Kidd, who made no attempt to conceal his deep dislike for Methodism and all its works, allowed his criticism to reach the stage where he voiced objection to Methodist children attending the National School on weekdays and their own school on Sundays.

Consequently, on 28th September, 1860, the foundation stone of the Wesleyan Methodist Day and Sunday School was laid on the site in Whitechapel Street. The building, which was largely financed by James Heald of Parrs Wood, was opened in May, 1861, when thirty-seven children presented themselves. The master was Mr. H. A. Johnstone, assisted by a sewing mistress, Sarah Peacock. In January, 1870, Mr. James Henry Killingbeck succeeded Mr. Johnstone and held the post for upwards of twenty years.

The year 1842, saw an important addition to Didsbury's educational establishments. The centenary of Wesleyan Methodism occurred in 1839. To commemorate the occasion a centenary fund was instituted, from the proceeds of which the large house on Wilmslow Road, formerly known as the Pump House, was purchased by thirty-two trustees in 1841. Wings were added at each side, thus making a U shaped building, and the entire edifice was faced with stone. At a later stage another wing was added at the back, this giving the building, which we now know as the Didsbury College of Education, its present appearance.

On its completion, in 1842, the building was used as a college for the preparation of candidates for the Wesleyan ministry, much to the annoyance of Rev. Kidd! The number of students was originally thirty-six who undertook a three year couse. The senior tutors were Rev. John Bowers, the principal, Rev. Dr. John Hannah, the theological tutor and Rev. William Thorpe, the classical tutor.

There can be little doubt that the selection of the site for the college was at the instigation of James Heald. He himself was among the original trustees, as were also Rev. Bowers and Rev. Hannah. Very shortly afterwards he purchased the land at the rear for his own use.

Except for periods when it was used as a military hospital in both World Wars the college building continued in use by the Methodists until 1951, when it was acquired by Manchester Corporation. As the Didsbury College of Education its association with education is ensured for as far as we can see into the future. Pupil teachers come from far beyond the boundaries of Manchester to study within its walls.

After the acquisition of the building by Manchester Corporation the Wesleyan training college moved to Bristol where it still retains the name Didsbury College.

Chapter X

SOME DIDSBURY FAMILIES

Of the very early inhabitants of Didsbury and its vicinity very little is known. The earliest reference we have to them is in a land transfer of 1196 whereby Richard le Norreis exchanged land in Heaton Norris for land in Bradford belonging to his brother, Jordan le Norreis. We thus make the acquaintance of the Norris family, whose name appears repeatedly in the annals of the district right up to modern times. We meet them again in the Survey of 1322 when one Robert le Norreis was the owner of a house and one oxgang of land in Heaton Norris for which he paid the lord of the Manor of Manchester 16d yearly. He also held 2½ acres nearby at a place called Rysumbridge, for which he paid the lord 6d each Christmas. He was probably the same person as the Robert le Norreis mentioned in the Exchequer Lay Subsidy Rolls in 1322. The mentions of the family name in the parish register, beginning in 1573 were legion.

Heaton Norris was the traditional home of the family, but they did not derive their name from it. On the contrary, there is every reason to suppose that it derived its name from them. We find William Norris, yeoman, living there in 1593, with Alice, his wife. In addition there were Robert, Edward, William and Katherine Norris there, who were probably their children. Robert had a large family, as did Ralph, one of his sons. There is no record of the family living outside Heaton Norris until the end of the seventeenth century, when they were to be found in Burnage, Green End, Withington and Fallowfield. By the early part of the eighteenth century we find them attracted by the rapid development of Manchester and Salford. In 1713 Robert and Mary Norris were living in Salford. In 1735 Robert Norris was in Ardwick and 1744 William Norris was in Chorlton-on-Medlock. At the end of the eighteenth century and the beginning of the nineteenth John Norris was living at Baguley. It is unfortunately not possible to trace the pedigree with any hope of accuracy, for like so many other families they had favourite Christian names. Between 1713 and 1753 no less than seven persons called Robert Norris were buried at Didsbury. Three of them were sons of fathers also called Robert Norris, all of whom lived at Heaton Norris. The names William and Katherine were also much used.

Coming to more modern times we find that, in 1832, Samuel Norris was an overseer of the poor and also constable of the township of Withington. He was probably the person of the same name who, in 1845, was the tenant of Pytha Fold Farm, the location of which is now marked by Pytha Fold Road. In 1847 one James Norris was in business as a saddler in Didsbury village. Born in 1819, he was the son of Samuel Norris, perhaps the same person as was the overseer of the poor and constable. A pillar of Methodism, and one of its pioneers in Didsbury, he was for many years a superintendent of the Wesleyan Methodist Day and Sunday School until his retirement in 1879. He died in 1880. His son, James Harold Norris, who died in 1922, was also a superintendent of the school. At the end of the nineteenth century he was the rate collector of Withington U.D.C., the assistant overseer of the poor of the township of Didsbury and the local Registrar of Births and Deaths. He was the founder of J. H. Norris & Son, estate agents, in which firm his grandsons are partners to-day.

Several very old families are still represented in Didsbury; the Rudds, the Hampsons and the Chorltons, but none can hope to compete with the Norris's for the length of time they can show their roots to have been in the district.

It was towards the end of the fifteenth century that reference was first made to the family of Janney, Janny, Jannie or Janne, who appear to have flourished in the South Manchester area until the beginning of the seventeenth century. Although there was no direct reference at all to the family in Didsbury there were a number of references in the parish register and elsewhere to persons of the name in Rusholme and Northenden. There was also reference to one Richard Janney of Withington.

The Janney family were clearly people of some standing. They appear to have enjoyed the confidence of the lords of the manors of both Withington and Northenden. When, in 1539, Ralph Longford sold the island in the Mersey to Robert Tatton he appointed one John Janney to attend as his agent to hand the land over, and when the same Robert Tatton led an armed raid on the water mill near Barlow Hall one of his lieutenants was a William Janne.

It is tempting to identify the Janneys with the family of Yannis, who were prominent in Didsbury in the seventeenth and eighteenth centuries. They appear to have been a family of more than average status and education. In 1660 Hugh Yannis was a churchwarden of the Manchester Collegiate Church, a fact recorded in the registers of Didsbury. The Didsbury churchwardens' accounts mentioned that in both 1673 and 1681 a Mr. Yannes, presumably the minister of a neighbouring church, preached in the chapel. The will of Hugh Yannis of Knutsford, made in 1777, mentioned Rev. William Twyford, the then minister of Didsbury, as a relative.

114

That the Yannisses were substantial farmers is beyond question. No family received greater mention in place names and field names. Yannis's Farm, which was probably the later name for the building called Yannes House, was on the same land as now accommodates the Philip Godlee Lodge. Yannis's Twenty Acres was on the site of Parkfield Road. Yannis's Intack was in the neighbourhood of where Adria Road and Veronica Road are. Yannis's Rye Hey was adjacent to the river near the point where Palatine Road now crosses it. Yannis New Field and Yannis Car were in the vicinity of where Parrs Wood Railway Station and Didsbury Cricket Ground lie. Yannis Field was probably where Lancaster Road meets Dene Road. Yannis Meadow was part of Withington Golf Course. Yannis Acre was one of the low lying fields at the bottom of Millgate Lane. The distribution of these places, in almost every part of the township, suggests that they were not all farmed by the same person. On the contrary, their number suggests that the family of Yannis was a large one.

Yet in view of their obvious number and prominence such references to the family as have come down to us are amazingly few, and all of those which show members of the family as living in Didsbury relate to the short period between 1660 and 1686. Furthermore only two households can be identified, those of Hugh Yannis and John Yannis. There was, it is true, an entry in the parish register referring to the marriage, in 1736, of Rev. Samuel Townson of Oldham and Alice Yannis of nearby Crompton but Miss Yannis's reason for coming to Didsbury to be married was, no doubt, connected with the fact that the minister was a relative of hers. This entry gives us the only reliable clue we have of the origins of the family. It is known from other sources that there was a family of Yannis in Oldham at the time and it is possibly more than coincidence that the name of Hugh, which was also borne by one of the two Didsbury Yannisses, was popular among them also.

The possibility that the Yannisses and the Janneys were of the same family is by no means to be ruled out. But if such was the case then it is indeed curious that between 1638 and 1660 there was no mention whatever of either name, although the parish registers were quite comprehensive over those years. They were not mentioned in the Protestation Returns of 1642 nor in the assessment for Poor Rate of 1655. As occupiers of land they would certainly have been mentioned in the rating assessment if they had been in the district.

If the Janneys left the district permanently and the Yannisses arrived later then there is nothing except a similarity in spelling to connect the two families. Yet could it be that they were the same family and that for some reason, connected with the Civil War, they left Didsbury at the beginning of that struggle, in 1642, and returned at the time of the restoration of Charles II on 1660? Could it indeed be that during those troubled times they took refuge in a foreign country where the spelling of their name was distorted? Who can tell?

It has been suggested that the family was the same family as the Gymney family of Chorlton. The name may eventually have been corrupted to Annis, Guiness or even Jones, but one thing is certain, the names Janney and Yannis are both now unknown in Didsbury, Oldham and everywhere else in England.

A family who took a prominent part in Didsbury life in the seventeenth and eighteenth centuries were the Twyfords. The only member of the family living there in the sixteenth century, from whom all the others were descended, was Ralph Twyford, who died in 1600. Nothing is known of when he arrived in Didsbury or from whence he came except that he was a resident of the district in 1573. He had three children, John, Martha and Richard. Richard Twyford had one son, Francis, but what became of either of them we have no record. John Twyford had seven children. He must have been considered among the gentry of the district since his youngest son, Richard, married Margaret Tatton, one of the family whose home was Wythenshaw Hall and who were lords of the manor of Northenden.

Richard Twyford and his elder brother, Robert, were among the defenders of the hall when it was besieged by Colonel Robert Dukinfield and a force of Parliamentary soldiers between 1642 and 1644. After the war their estates were confiscated by Parliament for their parts in this escapade, but they were allowed to redeem them by substantial fines. The papers relating to these proceedings show that Richard Twyford owned a rentcharge of £13 per annum payable out of land at Haughton. Robert Twyford must have been a substantial farmer. He had a share in the tenancies of two farms, one of which was Hulme's Tenement. He also had the tenancies of a farm called Coop's Tenement and fields called Pillockhey and Moorefields. All these were in Didsbury, although it is impossible to say precisely where.

This Robert Twford had three children, Sarah, Robert and Anne. The exalted position occupied by the family is evidenced by the fact that when the younger Robert was baptized, in 1662, he was described as the son of Robert Twyford, Gentleman. The eldest of the younger Robert's five sons, who was also called Robert, took holy orders and upon the resignation of Rev. Francis Hooper in 1726 was nominated as minister of Didsbury Chapel by Lady Ann Bland, the lord of the manor, who had recently acquired the right of patronage. He married Mary, one of the daughters of Harry Bancroft of Heaton Norris, and died in 1747. During the last few years of his life he held the Chapel of Birch in Rusholme as well as that of Didsbury. He was succeeded as minister of both chapels by his son, Rev. William Twyford B.A. of St. John's College, Cambridge. In 1745 William Twyford married Mollie Broome who must, presumably, have been one of the family of lawyers who provided the stewards of the Manor of Withington and were very soon to purchase almost the whole of Didsbury from the impoverished Sir John Bland. Unfortunately there is no record of her birth in the parish register and it is not therefore possible to say from which of the Broome family she was descended. William Twyford died in 1795 having then been minister of Didsbury for nearly 50 years.

116

Further evidence of the affluent position of the Twyfords is afforded by the fact that they were freeholders at a time when to be such was a sure sign of wealth. As early as 1733 we find Rev. Robert Twyford the owner of land now lying at Broome Croft, Simon Playing Fields, Withington Golf Course, Lancaster Road and Didsbury Refuse Tip. In all probability their home was on the present site of Broome Croft.

Towards the end of the eighteenth century the family seem to have spread out from Didsbury. In 1762 a William Twyford was living at Timperley and a little later reference was made to a Manchester merchant called Robert Twyford. Nevertheless the family did not all leave Didsbury. In 1824 the landlord of the Cock Inn, now known as the Olde Cock, was Miss Ann Twyford. The name is not extinct in South Manchester in our own time.

The name of Broome is carved deep into Didsbury's history. In 1720 we find one William Broome, of Chorlton, in the position of steward to Lady Ann Bland. How and when the family came to Didsbury we cannot be certain but the Protestation Return shows one John Boome (sic) living in Levenshulme in 1642 and the parish register contained references to Broomes living in the same place at the end of the seventeenth century. There was even a mention of one Joan Broome being married in Didsbury as early as 1595.

William Broome died in 1736 leaving three sons, Richard, the eldest, who was a Manchester attorney, John, who was a Manchester merchant and William, who seems to have succeeded him as steward of the manor and was probably an attorney also. As we have seen the improvident mode of life adopted by Lady Ann Bland's grandson, Sir John Bland, necessitated the sale of his Lancashire estates. Those in Didsbury and Withington he sold to the Broomes. The main purchase appears to have taken place at the end of January, 1753, when Richard Broome, the attorney, was the purchaser. For some reason which is not apparent he did not purchase the lands direct from Sir John. Instead he appointed a nominee, John Moss, who bought them with money he provided and transferred them to him the very day after he acquired them. There appears to have been another purchase at about the same time, when Richard and William Broome purchased together, but it is quite certain that by 1758 Richard Broome was the sole owner of much the major part of Withington and Didsbury. In that year he sold land comprising no less than twenty farms and a number of small holdings, mostly in Withington, to Samuel Egerton of Tatton Park, the purchase price being what in those days was the astronomical sum of £20,000. In the same year he sold much of his Didsbury property to his brother, William, for £5,113. After these sales Richard Broome owned the whole of what is now Fielden Park, a great stretch of land between Barlow Moor Road and Nell Lane, a large area in the vicinity of Christ Church, almost all the land at the bottom of Parrs Wood Road and the area in the vicinity of Kingsway, south of Wilmslow Road, as well as substantial areas made up of comparatively small holdings. William Broome's purchase from his brother included the

117

areas now covered by Clyde Road and Old Lansdowne Road, Parkfield Road and its neighbourhood, part of Fog Lane Park, Ballbrook Court, Didsbury College of Education, Didsbury Park. Parrs Wood Omnibus Depot, the allotments at the corner of Burnage Lane and Parrs Wood Lane, a stretch of land bounded by Fog Lane, Wilmslow Road and School Lane, parts of Withington Golf Course, Broome Croft, part, at least, of Simon Playing Fields, several fields in the vicinity of Dene Road and smaller tenements in the vicinity of Baldock Road and Northenden Bridge.

William Broome married Elizabeth, the youngest sister of Captain James Dawson, who is said to have been the hero of Shenstone's Ballad of Jemmy Dawson. He died in 1780, leaving three sons, William the younger, James and John. All this branch of the family were buried at Didsbury Chapel, where a wall plaque still records their history. James inherited the land in the vicinities of Clyde Road, Old Lansdowne Road and Parkfield Road. By 1795 he was insolvent and that land was conveyed to trustees for the benefit of his creditors. The land on the sites of Clyde Road and Old Lansdowne Road found its way into the hands of Samuel Brundrett, a Chorlton farmer, at whose death it was shared between his sons. The property near Parkfield Road was taken up by George Withington who built there a magnificent residence known as Parkfield.

William Broome, the younger, inherited most, if not all, of the rest of his father's estate. From him it descended to his son-in-law, Colonel John Parker. His ownership marked a turning point. To the Mosleys, the Blands and the Broomes the desire to keep land in the family was axiomatic. Colonel Parker, on the other hand, was essentially of the middle classes by whom the reins of power were now being seized not only in Didsbury but throughout the country. He felt himself bound by no such tradition. Whilst the lords of the manor had jealously guarded their land for centuries, selling only small parts of it, mostly near Didsbury Moor, he looked on it as nothing more than a form of investment to be sold when favourable apportunity presented itself. Shortly after William Broome's death he was actually seeking purchasers. Much of his estate was purchased in various lots by the families of Heald, Souchay, Beaver and Slater, most of whom were middle class families enriched by the Industrial Revolution.

William Broome, the younger, who became a Justice of the Peace, died without issue on 13th August, 1810. His wife, Mary, survived him until 18th January, 1815.

Richard Broome, the brother of William Broome, the elder, was succeeded by four children: Joseph, who appears to have died within a few years of him; Ann, who lived at Yannis's Farm, which stood on the site of Philip Godlee Lodge; Frances, who married Rev. James Bayley, one of a pre-eminent family of landowners, who lived in the vicinity of Cotton Lane and Mary, who became the wife of Henry ffeilden of New Inn, Westminster. By his will, made in 1760, he left the bulk of his estate to Joseph. Joseph died intestate, his property being taken in equal shares by his sisters, Ann Broome and Frances Bayley, and his grandson, Robert

Feilden, who took the share which would have been taken by his mother, Mary, who was also dead.

The Feilden family originated in Blackburn, where, in 1480, Henry ffeilden was appointed a trustee for the management and appropriation of certain lands bequeathed for the purpose of establishing a chantry and chantry priest for the parish church, and his son, Randle ffeilden, was appointed by Royal Charter, in 1567, as one of the original governors of Blackburn Grammar School.

Robert ffeilden, who was descended from the above-named, moved to Manchester in the early part of the eighteenth century. In his will he described himself as a Manchester merchant although he still owned land in Blackburn. He was clearly a man of substance, a fact demonstrated not only by his ownership of land but by a legacy of £2,000 which he bequeathed to his daughter, Ann. He was the father of Henry ffeilden who, as we have seen, married Mary Broome. In the published pedigree of the family his address was shown as Didsbury Hall; a misnomer, since no building of that name existed. What was meant was Didsbury House, on the site of Viceroy Court.

Henry ffeilden's only son, was Robert Feilden, a barrister, of the Inner Temple, who later lived at Didsbury House and Runcorn. It will be observed that the son spelled his name with a capital "F" as did his successors, as distinct from the father who used the small "ff" which had been used by his ancestors for centuries.

As we have seen Mary ffeilden's share of her father's estate was taken by Robert Feilden, who also inherited the share of Ann Broome, whose heir he was, when she died in 1819. The share of Frances Bayley had been settled and Robert Feilden acquired it also after her death, which took place in 1818. Thus the original estate of Richard Broome was united again in the hands of his grandson.

Robert Feilden was married twice; first to Ann Mosley, eldest daughter of Sir John Parker Mosley, lord of the Manor of Manchester, who died in 1810, and secondly to Sarah White. He also took up residence in Didsbury House, where he lived until his death in 1830 and where his widow lived on until her own death twenty years later. He was buried in Didsbury churchyard on the north side of the church, where his gravestone can still be seen.

During his lifetime Robert Feilden purchased the advowson of the Rectory of Bebington, that is to say the right to nominate the incumbent of that parish. We do not know what price was paid but such was the importance attached, in those days, to a right of presentation that it must have been substantial, since he, wealthy landowner though he was, was unable to purchase it outright and had to discharge the purchase price over a period. His reason for purchasing it was to provide a living for the eldest of his four sons, Robert Mosley Feilden, who was in holy orders, and whom he eventually nominated to the curacy. By his will he left his Didsbury estates to Robert Mosley Feilden, who was married to Frances Mary, daughter of a Major General Ramsey. Robert Mosley Feilden's

119

attitude to the estate was the same as had been that of his remote relative, Colonel Parker. The process of selling off was resumed. Broad Oak Farm was sold to John Cookson and Lapwing Hall Farm to Henry Bury, a director of the Manchester and Liverpool Banking Company. On the death of Sarah Feilden, Didsbury House was sold to George Robinson, a cotton manufacturer, of Longsight. Plots of land at The Beeches and near Lancaster Road were sold to estate developers in whatever shapes best suited them. Robert Mosley Feilden died in 1862. It was him to whom Fletcher Moss was referring when he complained that much of the land in Didsbury was owned by a clergyman although the church got none of it.

Robert Mosley Feilden left four sons, Robert Feilden, a lieutenant colonel in the 44th Regiment of Foot, George Ramsey Feilden, who succeeded him as Rector of Bebington, Henry Broome Feilden, a lieutenant colonel in the 6th Regiment of Foot and Oswald Mosley Feilden who became Rector of Welsh-Frankton. The two soldier sons both served in the Crimea and were present at the siege of Sebastopol, Henry Broome Feilden being thrice wounded. The Didsbury estates were inherited by the eldest son, Col. Robert Feilden, who lived at Dulas Court, Hereford, a residence purchased by his father. He lost little time in disposing of what remained of them. Part of the area which we now know as Fielden Park was sold first, in 1866. Small plots in the vicinity of Osborne Street were sold to builders in 1865. In 1868 the entire Millgate Estate was put up for auction and purchased by James Ryder for £12,100. Eventually the last fragment was sold. It has not been ascertained where this was but it may have been the land which is now the site of Fielden Road. It is ironic that the name of this road, meant to perpetuate the memory of a family once so important in the area, is mis-spelt as also is that of Fielden Park. The name was Feilden, not Fielden.

How typical the Feildens were of the rising middle class families of their day. Drawn to Manchester by the calls of commerce they intermarried with the family of the very lords of the manor by whom their ancestors, the Broomes, had been employed. The pursuit of trade they grew to regard as vulgar, turning instead to the bar, the church and the army; professions which, in those times, were regarded as the preserves of the gentry.

After the Blands, the Broomes and the Feildens the next most substantial landowning family of the eighteenth and early nineteenth centuries were the Bamford Heskeths, although they never made their home in the district.

In 1746 John Davenport of Stockport executed his will whereby he left all his Cheshire and Lancashire estates to three ladies whom he referred to as "my Cousins Bamfords". These ladies, Margaret, Ann and Susan Bamford, were of a family living at Bamford, near Rochdale, from which place they took their name. They were daughters of William Bamford and relatives of William Bamford who was High Sheriff of Lancashire in 1787. One of their ancestors, William Bamford of Bamford had been a freeholder in the county as early as 1600.

120

Included in John Davenport's Lancashire estates were substantial holdings in Didsbury, lying in various parts of the district. How John Davenport acquired this land we cannot be certain, although it seems that he obtained a great deal of it from William and Catherine Tatton of Wythenshawe at some time between 1734 and 1746. It is known also that, in 1384, Nicholas and Cecilia de Baumford made a settlement of estates consisting of two messuages, forty-four acres of land, four acres of meadow and two acres of pasture in Manchester and Withington. In this context Withington would be the Manor of Withington, which included Didsbury. The possibility that they were ancestors of the Bamford family cannot be ruled out. If such was the case then doubtless John Davenport, who was a cousin of the family, inherited the estates.

Susan Bamford predecessed John Davenport, leaving her sisters, Ann and Margaret, who by then was married to one George Bamforth, to take John Davenport's estate in equal shares. Margaret Bamforth made her will in August, 1773, leaving all her property to her surviving sister. By 1777 she too had died, leaving Ann Bamford in possession of all John Davenport's original estates.

Ann Bamford was related to a Robert Hesketh and during her lifetime she entailed her estates in favour of him and his descendants, confirming this settlement by her will, which was dated 26th October, 1778. By this will she also left £100 for the benefit of poor housekeepers in Stockport, Cheadle-Hulme and Didsbury, not receiving Poor Relief, £50 to the trustees of the Lunatic Hospital in Manchester for the use of that charity and £50 to the newly established Infirmary at Manchester.

It was a common custom in those days for wealthy people to stipulate in their wills that the persons inheriting their estates were to adopt their surnames and arms. This condition seems to have been imposed by Ann Bamford, and by 1800, shortly after her death, we find Robert Hesketh and Lloyd Hesketh, his son, being known by the surname of Bamford. They must presumably have received some further legacy shortly afterwards from a member of their own family with a similar condition attached, for by 1813 they were known by the name of Bamford Hesketh. At about the same time Robert Bamford Hesketh acquired Gwrych Castle, near Abergele, North Wales, built in comparatively modern times in the style of the Plantaganet castles which are such a feature of that part of the country.

In 1878 Winifred Bamford Hesketh, who was either the grand-daughter or the great grand-daughter of Lloyd Bamford Hesketh, was engaged, at 19 years of age, to be married to the Honourable Douglas Mackinson Baillie Hamilton Cochran, commonly called Lord Cochran, the heir apparent of the Earl of Dundonald. As was usual, the bride's father executed a marriage settlement whereby the existing entail, presumably that created by Ann Bamford, was revoked and substantial estates, including Gwrych Castle and all the land in Didsbury belonging to the family, were settled on the young couple. It was provided that if the intended marriage took place Lord Cochran was to receive an annuity of

£2,000 per annum. Subject thereto Miss Bamford Hesketh was to receive the entire rents during her life. After her death they were to be paid to Lord Cochran. There were also the usual complicated provisions as to what was to happen to the trust fund after the death of both the husband and the wife.

The Earl of Dundonald died on 15th January, 1885, whereupon Lord and Lady Cochran assumed the titles of the Earl and Countess of Dundonald. The countess died on 16th January, 1924, and under the terms of the marriage settlement the earl succeeded to the lands formerly belonging to her family. Some of these lands, near Didsbury Park, remained in the settlement until the 1930's when they were sold to provide sites for Brayton Avenue, Marton Avenue and Dalston Drive.

The name of Winifred, Countess of Dundonald, is remembered in the names of three roads in Didsbury today, as that of the Bamford Hesketh family is remembered in two others. The name of Ladysmith Road is not of quite such obvious origin. It derives from the fact that the earl fought at Ladysmith during the South African War, which took place shortly before the road was laid out.

The Birley family is prominent in local affairs today as they have been for a century and a half. One tradition is that they derived their name from Bereclegh or Birclogh, in Balderstone, near Blackburn. Certain it is that the family were living in North Lancashire at an early date, although a rival tradition has it that they were of Irish origin, the name Boarlegh being there applied to one who destroyed wild boars. It is known that Walter Burley was born in 1274 and died in 1345 and in 1335 Adam de Burleye was witness to a judgement relating to the chancel of the church at Whalley.

The family traces its descent directly from John Birley, yeoman, of Poulton-le-Fylde, who was buried at that place in 1732. His son, John Birley de Birks, afterwards of Kirkham a West India merchant, who died in 1767, was the father of Richard Birley of Blackburn, who married Alice, eldest daughter of Hugh Hornby of Kirkham. They had three sons, all of whom became prominent in South Manchester. The eldest was John Birley, born on 30th August, 1775. He later lived at Platt Hall, Rusholme. The second was, Hugh Hornby Birley, born on 10th March, 1778. In 1819 Hugh Hornby Birley, then a major in the Manchester Yeomanry, was present at the Peterloo Massacre, the only connection which can be found to link Didsbury with that notorious event. In 1822 he was tried at Lancaster Assizes, jointly with Richard Withington, captain, Alexander Oliver, private, and Edward Meogher, trumpeter in the same regiment. He married Cicely, daughter of Thomas Hornby of Kirkham and lived at Broome House. Later he moved to Pendleton, Salford, to a house which he also named Broome House. He was a Deputy Lieutenant for the County of Lancaster. His brother, Joseph Birley, the third son of Richard Birley was also a Deputy Lieutenant and also married a daughter of Thomas Hornby of Kirkham. Thus two brothers married two sisters. Joseph Birley purchased a large estate in the vicinity of the present Dene

Road in or about 1820 and built on it a mansion house, known as Ford Bank, which stood approximately where Fordbank Road is today. He acted as his own architect. He was the father of no less than eleven sons and six daughters. The fifth son, Hugh Birley, who lived at Moorland, which stood where Mere Drive, Fog Lane, now lies was Member of Parliament for Manchester between 1868 and his death in 1883. A pillar of the Church of England, Joseph Birley was a churchwarden of Didsbury in 1823. Many of the church's causes benefitted from his generosity. In 1823 he gave £20 towards the cost of extending the churchyard, in 1841 £75 for the erection of St. Paul's Church, Withington, and, in 1843 another £150 for the extension of the Church school in School Lane.

The sixth son of Joseph Birley, and the brother of Hugh Birley M.P., was Herbert Birley J.P. of Spring Bank, Pendleton. For a lifetime he interested himself in education. In 1865, Rev. W. J. Kennedy, one of Her Majesty's Inspectors, writing about elementary education in Lancashire, observed:-

> "The work of one gentleman in particular is beyond all human praise for what he is doing. I mean Herbert Birley, Esq. of Manchester with whose generous educational work I constantly meet in that city."

On the formation of the Manchester School Board, in 1870, Herbert Birley was elected its chairman, and on 11th June, 1874, he laid the foundation stone of Vine Street School, Hulme, the first school that the Board erected. In 1871 he inaugurated a free meals scheme for poor children in the Board Schools.

He was the father of Joseph Harold Birley, who made his home at Stonecroft, at the corner of Parkfield Road and Elm Road. The latter married Edith Gladys Fernandes Lewis, who, despite advancing years, is still a prominent member of the Manchester Education Committee.

No account of the families of Didsbury would be complete without reference to the Heald family of Parrs Wood. But first a word of caution, it is commonly thought, in the district, that this family is related to the proprietors of A. Heald Ltd., the well-known firm of dairymen. In fact this is not so.

The Healds did not build Parrs Wood, the Georgian mansion which stands in the angle now formed by Kingsway and Parrs Wood Lane. It was erected at some time prior to the year 1795 by William Boardman, who was subsequently made bankrupt. In 1825 it was purchased by James Heald.

Didsbury has had no resident more worthy than James Heald. Born in 1796 at Portwood, near Stockport, the second son of James Heald of Brinnington and Disley, he followed his father into the family business of cotton merchants. Although born into a Methodist family his early intention was to enter the ministry of the Church of England and he relinquished his commercial interests to devote himself to study for that purpose. However, through the influence of an uncle, he returned to the Wesleyan fold and devoted himself enthusiastically to its interests. He was treasurer of the Wesleyan Missionary Society, and one of the original trustees of the Methodist Training College, for which the building which now houses the Didsbury College of Education was erected. Indeed it was probably he who suggested Didsbury as the home of the college, which stood within easy walking distance of his home. In his day he was, and has been described as, the most prominent layman in the Methodist connexion. He was the founder of Stockport Infirmary, which he liberally endowed, and was a pioneer of the Sunday school movement in the north of England. The Didsbury Wesleyan Methodist Day and Sunday School was built with funds which he largely provided.

In 1847 he was returned to the House of Commons by Stockport as an Independent Conservative member, a rare banner for a Nonconformist to fight under in those days. In Parliament he found full scope for his philanthropic zeal. He was closely associated with Benjamin Disraeli in the latter's reforming policies, particularly in relation to the hours of employment for children, where, especially considering his own business interests, he had very advanced views. He was an enthusiast also for the improvement of industrial relations and the legal recognition of the trade unions. In those fields also he found a mighty ally in Disraeli. After only five very productive years in Parliament he was unseated, in 1852, when he declared himself in favour of free trade.

He died at Parrs Wood on 20th October, 1873, and was buried at Chapel-en-le-Frith, Derbyshire. After his death Sir Joseph Napier described his character as a rare combination of evangelical earnestress and wise moderation.

He was survived by his devoted sister, Margaret. Parrs Wood and its estates he left to his nephew, William Norris Heald. Shortly after his death his sister and nephew erected St. Paul's Methodist Church, in the grounds of the college, in his memory.

William Norris Heald took no apparent interest in politics. He was an outdoors man. He achieved more than a local reputation as a sportsman, and the standard of his farming at Parrs Wood was regarded as exemplary. His family still treasure medals he won in agricultural shows with his bulls.

Although a Methodist he was the patron of a number of church livings, including that of Didsbury, which he purchased, in 1879, for the sum of £1,500. For this his neighbour, Fletcher Moss, did not lightly forgive him. Although he did not mention Heald by name he launched vicious criticisms, the target of which was obvious. Writing, in 1890, in "Didsbury; Sketches, Reminiscences and Legends" he declared:-

> "It is a scandal and a disgrace, sanctioned by the law, for a rich man (perhaps a dissenter) to buy up the right to nominate the rector of a church, and to ignore the wishes of many who worshipped in that church before he was born."

And again:-

"We are told that the Church of England is a national church, and that the priests of it have a special grace, derived from the laying on of hands . . . If so, how is it . . . a dissenter may buy the power to nominate his choice of a "successor of the Apostles?""

How typical it was of the charitable disposition of his family that Heald bore no malice to the author of these attacks. A few years after the words were published Fletcher Moss stood in Didsbury as a candidate for the Withington U.D.C. The names of W. N. Heald J.P. and James Heald, his son, were prominently displayed on his election literature as declared supporters.

William Norris Heald moved from Parrs Wood to Southport before the First World War so as to get sea air for the chest complaint from which he suffered. By that time Parrs Wood had lost much of its charm, first to the Midland Railway Company, which owned the sunken line from Stockport to Didsbury and later to the London and North Western Railway Company, which owned the elevated line to Wilmslow.

In 1895 W. N. Heald made a gift of much of the land surrounding the big house to his son, James Heald, a Manchester solicitor, who lived at Ellerslie, 19, Didsbury Park, now known as Ellerslie Guest House. James Heald was much interested in the local organisation of the Conservative Party. He built, and owned the Didsbury Conservative Club and was chairman of the Stretford Conservative Association when Mr. C. A. Cripps, later Lord Parmoor, and father of Sir Stafford Cripps, was High Tory Member of Parliament for that constituency. He was married to Nettie Steward Brown, one of a well known family of Liverpool, to which city he moved after his retirement from legal practice in 1909. He very soon joined Liverpool Corporation and when Didsbury Library was declared open on 15th May, 1915, he was present as Chairman of the Liverpool Libraries Committee.

James Heald died in 1921, leaving his wife and two sons, William Henry Arthur Heald and Lionel Frederick Heald, surviving him.

Lionel Frederick Heald, who was born at Ellerslie on 7th August, 1897, took to the bar as his profession. There his natural talents and capacity for work took him to the top. After becoming a King's Counsel, at the remarkably early age of 40 he was returned as Member of Parliament for Chertsey, Surrey, in 1950, using part of the first James Heald's Election Address! He was appointed Attorney General by Sir Winston Churchill in his second administration in 1951, receiving the accolade of knighthood at the same time. He resigned from office in 1954 but remained in Parliament as a back-bencher. He served in both World Wars; in the first in the Royal Engineers and in the second in the Royal Air Force, where he became an Air Commodore on appointment to General Eisenhower's staff.

Sir Lionel Heald is indeed a local boy who made good. It is a matter of wonder that few Didsbury people are aware that so distinguished a figure was born among them, grew up among them and cherishes his memories of them. In a charming letter to the author Sir Lionel observed "It seems strange now, but in the years from 1900 that I can remember Didsbury was still rural."

The Heald family had started to sell off their Didsbury lands at the end of the nineteenth century, but they retained much until the 1930's, when they were sold to provide sites for some of the semi-detached residences which abound in East Didsbury.

Chapter XI

THE 19TH CENTURY AND AFTER

During the first half of the nineteenth century Didsbury changed comparatively little. The Agricultural Revolution brought in improved methods of farming which meant that the small enclosures, so much in evidence in the eighteenth century, were considered to be uneconomical and were merged into larger units. This was particularly so in the case of the fields adjacent to the main road. Thus four small fields known as Famous Pits, Cockshut, Clarks and Bolton Wood Croft, at the corner of Parrs Wood Lane, then known as Bolton Wood Gate Lane, and Burnage Lane, then probably known as Slate Lane, became united into one field called Famous Pits. Between Parrs Wood House and the Mersey Moor Bank, Moor Bank Meadow, Patch, Great Meadow and Meer Bank were merged together as Mersey Meadow and in the present vicinity of Didsbury Park Wood's Townfield, Clerk's Illbeard, Wood's Illbeard, the Croft, Salt Rooks and Walker's Illbeard became two fields known as Middle Paddock and Further Paddock. On the other hand, in those parts of the township which were not near a main road, and were therefore too inaccessable for arable farming, the same process did not take place. The area through which Palatine Road nowruns, just north of the river,looked exactly the same in 1850 as it had looked seventy or eighty years earlier, and indeed, just before the opening of Kingsway in the twentieth century, the fields of Broad Oak Farm were the same as they had been at the end of the eighteenth century.

There was relatively little building during the first fifty years after 1800. A palatial mansion house was built at some time before 1832 in Clerk's Moorfields and Yannis's Twenty Acres at what is now the corner of Parkfield Road and Elm Road. Known as Parkfield it was the home of George Withington. Its grounds stretched from the turnpike road to the boundary of Lapwing Hall Farm, near where Linden Road is now. When it was demolished, in 1909, the drive leading from Lapwing Lane to the house was widened and paved. We now know it as Elm Road.

The land at the corner of Fog Lane and the turnpike road which, it will be remembered, was part of the land formerly known as the Seven Intacks, was purchased in 1839 by John Daniel Souchay, a Manchester merchant, who erected there a fine house, distinguished by its very high gables, known as Eltville House. In 1888 this house, with eight acres of land, was acquired by James Clayton Chorlton for no less than £9,300. In 1931 Mr. Clayton sold the house and its lands and the present houses were built on the site. By that time the old house had become known as The Priory. The name of Chorlton is remembered in Clothorn Road. The word Clothorn is an anagram of Chorlton.

As we have seen, Ford Bank House was built at some date prior to 1821. It was sold in 1858 to Thomas Ashton, whose son, Thomas Gair Ashton, later Lord Ashton of Hyde, was Liberal M.P. for Hyde and entertained no less a person than W. E. Gladstone in the house. During the early part of the century Mrs. Ellen Markland lived at Didsbury Cottage, near where Lansdowne House stands now. On the site of Viceroy Court stood a fine house, known as Didsbury House, occupied by Mrs. Sarah Feilden, widow of Robert Feilden, until her death in 1850. Opposite Didsbury House, where The Limes now stands, was a small, but well appointed house, built about 1840 by Mrs. Ruth Offley. Philip Godlee Lodge was also built in the first half of the century. It was then known as Ramsdell House, but later as The Elms. It was the boyhood home of Fletcher Moss before his family moved into the Old Parsonage. It is not known whether the present Didsbury Hotel and Olde Cock belong to this period or not. What is known is that the Ring o'Bells, was sold to Samuel Bethel in 1821. Between that date and 1855 the new owner placed boundary stones round the village green, in front of the inn, and treated it as his own property. The community spirit had so declined in the village that nobody stopped him. He sold the inn and its grounds, including the green, in 1855 to Thomas Crompton, but by then he had changed its name to the Church Inn.

On and near the site of The Grove was a group of houses, one of which, later No. 813 Wilmslow Road, was built in the style of a previous age, leading many to think that it was Georgian. It was, in fact, built between 1843 and 1845 and was demolished in 1968. Willow Bank, in Millgate Lane, was owned and occupied by Dr. William Wood, the village doctor. The old houses at the corner of Millgate Lane and Wilmslow Road were also built in the period we are considering. Broomcroft Hall was built in 1847 by William Hobbs, a wealthy Manchester manufacturer. A water mill was erected in 1810 near where Kingsway crosses the river.

Apart from these developments Didsbury looked very much the same place in 1850 as it had been in 1800, but all that was changed by the opening of Palatine Road. The credit for this project must go to Mr. Henry Bury, the banker, who lived at Moorfield, a house which stood approximately where Ballbrook Avenue now joins St. Aldwyns Road, although its grounds stretched as far as the Wilmslow Road. Lord Egerton of Tatton gave the land for the road between Withington village and Lapwing Lane. Henry Bury himself gave the land between Lapwing Lane and Barlow Moor Road, then known as Barlow Moor Lane, taking good care that the road was laid along the extreme western boundary of his land, known as Lapwing Hall Farm. The farmhouse of this estate, which stood a few yards back from Lapwing Lane, had to be demolished to make way for the road. There is some reason to think that it may have been built more than 200 years before. Almost all the land for the road between Barlow Moor Lane and the Mersey was given by Mr. Robert Feilden, although a short stretch, alongside what is now Withington Golf Course, belonged to Mr. Rudd, a descendant of John Rudd, whom we have already met as a surveyor of the highways, and was purchased from him.

The road, with a girder bridge over the river, took one day under twelve months to complete. It was formally opened to traffic on 26th December, 1862, when twenty or more of the trustees of the Manchester and Wilmslow Turnpike Trust went along it in a procession of carriages, after which they attended a celebration at Mr. Bury's home. The total cost of making the road was in the region of £12,000, but when completed it was sold to the turnpike trustees for only £8,000. A toll gate was erected at the corner of the new road and Barlow Moor Lane but at first the road was so little used that during the first week the takings were less than the collector's wages.

As we have seen, Henry Bury and his neighbours sold the road for only two-thirds of the cost of its construction, but there was method in their folly. The new road opened up the inaccessable parts of the township. The value of the land on both sides increased enormously. Indeed when, in 1866, Robert Feilden sold the land on the east side of the road just south of Barlow Moor Lane it fetched a price of more than £500 per acre. This transaction alone more than compensated him for his share of the loss.

The land facing onto the road quickly came into high demand for building purposes. The first developers to realise its potentialities were, apparently, the trustees of the Rusholme and Withington Estate Benefit Building Society, who, while it was yet being constructed, contracted to purchase some 29 acres which are now the site of Clyde Road, Old Lansdowne Road and Cresswell Grove. For this they agreed to pay £8,700, representing £300 per acre. The arrangement made with the owner was that he was to receive the purchase money by monthly instalments and was only to convey the legal ownership of the land to the society when he had been paid in full. Meanwhile thirty-two members of the society agreed to take up the land, paying for it also by monthly instalments. In 1863 a plot of land fronting the new road was acquired by the society for £1,070.2.6., thus giving access to the land through what is now Queen's Road. The total paid by the society was therefore £9,770.2.6., while the total amount they received from their thirty-two members was £15,050. The main purchase was completed in 1865, whereupon the present houses were erected by the thirty-two purchasers.

The estate was named Albert Park, after the Prince Consort, who died in 1861.

Few people in Didsbury realise that the district was the scene of such early building society activity. As a matter of fact, Albert Park was not the first such scheme visualised for the district. In 1852 the British Freehold Land Society publicised a similar project for the area on both sides of what is now Kingston Road. This land was divided into 131 plots, which were to be allocated to members of the society at the rate of one plot per share. Shares cost up to £40 each and could be purchased by subscriptions of 4/- per month. It was proposed to hold a ballot to determine priority of allotment. The society originally intended to demolish the old cottages, now Nos. 15 and 17 Millgate Lane, and also to build on the land on the east side of Kingston Road, which now forms part of the grounds of the Shirley Institute, but for some reason the scheme was never put into effect. Nevertheless a reminder of it is still there to be seen, for Kingston Road and Kingston Avenue are laid exactly in the positions visualised when it was drawn up.

The first name of the new turnpike road was Northenden New Road, but at the request of the postal authorities it was changed to Palatine Road. Building along it continued for some years. Fielden Park was laid out in 1869 and the large houses between Barlow Moor Road and Lapwing Lane were erected in the early 1870's.

From 1850 onwards Didsbury changed fast under the influence of its growing neighbour, Manchester. By 1859 Rev. Robert Mosley Feilden was selling land to Leopold Schwabe on which to erect The Beeches and by 1865, his son, Col. Robert Feilden, was selling land for houses in the vicinity of Grove Street and Church Street.

The old building of the Shirley Institute, known as The Towers, was purchased by Daniel Adamson in 1875. This magnificent building became known as Calendar House, since it was said to have 12 towers, 52 rooms and 365 windows. Its claim to fame is that, in 1882, it was the place where seventy-six influential people met and formed a committee to further the idea of cutting a ship canal between Manchester and the mouth of the Mersey.

In 1864 Frederick Edward Gaddum purchased ten acres of land where Adria Road, Veronica Road, Gaddum Road and Atwood Road are now. On a spot in the centre of Adria Road he built a house, of comparatively modest proportions, which he called Adria House. The rest of the land he used as a garden with extensive lawns and shrubberies. There was even an artificial pond with a decorative bridge. The bulk of this holding was leased to Manchester Corporation, in 1923, for horticultural allotments, but by that time Adria House had been demolished.

Contemporaneously with these visible developments came sweeping changes in the structure of local government. We have seen how, in the eighteenth century, and indeed for most of the nineteenth, the townships were governed, if that can be deemed the correct expression, by the churchwardens, constables, surveyors of the highway, collectors and

130

assessors. Now, in 1876, there came local government in a form approaching that which we know today, for in that year was born the Withington Local Board of Health, set up under the various Public Health and Local Government Acts of the mid-nineteenth century. The first elections for the board, which comprised the townships of Burnage, Chorlton-cum-Hardy and Didsbury, with most of the township of Withington and part of Moss Side, was held in November, 1876, when fifteen members were elected. The mode of election was indeed curious when judged by modern standards. The district was not sub-divided into wards. Any would-be member of the board could nominate himself as a candidate. Not every voter had the same number of votes. Every house-owner or occupier had one vote for every £50 of rateable value up to a maximum of £300, but if he was both owner and occupier he had double the number of votes. Thus it was possible for the owner-occupier of a highly rated house to have twelve votes. There was no polling booth, but the voting papers were delivered to the voters three days before the election and collected later for counting.

The offices of the board were in the building, still known as Withington Town Hall, in Lapwing Lane, which was built for it in 1881. Despite its shortcomings the board did some good work. It certainly achieved much that the individual townships could not have done. In 1881 it purchased some low lying land on the banks of the Mersey, a little lower down the river from Jackson's Boat, Chorlton-cum-Hardy, for use as a sewage works. Today many people are puzzled why a site in Chorlton-cum-Hardy is known as Withington Sewage Works. In 1887 it arranged to share this sewage works with Levenshulme on agreed terms.

In 1890 it prosecuted a fried-fish dealer, carrying on business in Hardman Street, for causing what its Medical Officer, Dr. Hardman, described as "a concentrated stink", but the troublesome dealer won the case and his neighbours had to make the most of what they doubtless thought to be a bad job. A refuse tip, which the board opened in Palatine Road, was abandoned in the same year because of complaints from local residents—shades of things to come—and a refuse destructor was purchased and installed somewhere on the east side of Nell Lane, where it was considered to be far enough away from any centre of population to avoid complaints.

Finally, in 1893, the board purchased Didsbury's first recreation ground from the Executors of a Mr. Bolland for £2,500. This we now know as Didsbury Recreation Ground. The chairman of the committee responsible for laying it out was Fletcher Moss, who had been elected to the board in 1891, and who complained bitterly that he was allowed only £10 for the planting of the borders along the path leading to the recreation ground from Wilmslow Road.

The Local Boards of Health were swept away by the Local Governments Act, 1894, and replaced, in built-up areas, by Urban District Councils. So died the Withington Local Board, but relics of it can still be seen in the district. Its name appears, here and there, on street grids and a monogram, composed of the letters W.L.B., remains over the door of Withington Town Hall.

Shortly before it was abolished the area of Withington Local Board of Health was sub-divided into six wards, Withington, Fallowfield, Whalley Range, Chorlton-cum Hardy, Didsbury and West Didsbury. The original suggestion was that the last named ward should be called Albert Park and a controversy arose which was eventually resolved by appeal to the County Council. So hot did tempers become over the question that a writ for defamation was issued by a member of the board, Mr. Coombs, who was also the landlord of the Midland Hotel, Lapwing Lane. When the case was heard he was awarded damages of one farthing!

The existing wards were taken over by Withington Urban District Council, which covered the same area as the Local Board had done, except that it lost the small piece of Moss Side. Three councillors were elected for each ward. The first three elected for Withington were Mr. Coombs and Messrs. J. Bradshaw and W. E. Harwood. Those for Didsbury were Messrs. R. C. Raby, J. Moore and Fletcher Moss.

The Urban District Council seems to have been resolved to oppose any and every measure which could be thought of as progressive. In 1892, and again in 1895, Fletcher Moss proposed the adoption of the Public Libraries Act, 1892, but was defeated on both occasions. It is true that in 1895, on the motion of Councillor Raby, a committee was appointed to consider the question of free libraries and baths for the district but it certainly did not build a library. For that Didsbury had to wait until 1908, when one was inaugurated in a room rented from Mrs. Henry Simon, mother of the future Lord Simon of Wythenshawe. In 1915 the present fine building, erected with money provided by Andrew Carnegie, after a personal approach by Fletcher Moss, was opened.

As regards the public baths, the Council decided, in 1896, to defer the question indefinitely. It was considered again in August of the same year but no action was ordered to be taken. The baths in Burton Road were not opened until 1911, after incorporation with Manchester.

In 1895 the Manchester Suburban Electric Supply Company gave notice to the Council of its intention to apply to Parliament for a Provisional Order to supply electricity to the district. Even this was opposed by the Council. Subsequently a resolution was moved to set up a sub-committee to consider the desirability of applying for similar powers for the Council itself. This was not carried, but it was decided to hold a ballot to see whether the voters of the district wanted electricity or whether they did not. It is hard for us, more than seventy years later, to realise that barely half of those who voted were in favour of having an electricity supply and agreeable to using it if it was brought to them.

But the expansion of Manchester was proceeding at ever-increasing speed, and by the beginning of the twentieth century the tide had passed through Didsbury. Yet although, to all outward appearances, it had become merged in the great city it still had no School Board, no library and no public baths. Even more important there was no fire engine or hose reel in the whole of the Urban District, and the shortest time it took a fire-engine from Manchester to reach a fire in the district was fifteen minutes. The people of Withington had to pay more than the Mancunians for their water and gas which Manchester supplied. The services provided by Manchester were, in some measure, paid for by the people of Withington, and indeed the Manchester tramways, which ran at a profit, partly derived from the services provided in Withington, was able to pay a portion of it towards the relief of the City rates.

In the circumstances it is not surprising that it was increasingly being felt in the Urban District that the time was ripe for amalgamation with Manchester. There now came on the scene a remarkable body called the Amalgamation League, founded on 20th May, 1902. It is not known who its founder was but the secretary, from the moment of its inception, was Mr. I. R. Dixon, of 16 Leopold Avenue, West Didsbury. On 21st July Mr. Thomas Eggington J.P., of West Didsbury, was enrolled as a member. He immediately assumed a role of leadership. At first the League had no premises, and indeed, on 13th August, 1902, a meeting of the General Committee was held, incredible as it may seem, in an empty house, No. 22 Leopold Avenue. Later temporary accommodation was obtained at No. 4 Cavendish Road.

At the meeting of 13th August the rules of the League were settled. The objects were "to call public attention to the advantages to be derived by this district becoming amalgamated within the boundaries of the City of Manchester". It was provided that a committee of 12 members was to be elected in each of the six wards, but by the time of the first annual report no ward had been able to provide more than eight. Indeed Fallowfield had only been able to find two, although the report claimed, rather optimistically, that the committees would be brought up to their full complement in due course. Not all the committee men were asked to consent before they were elected and some of them were not even subscribers. At no time did the League have more than thirty-eight members.

On 7th August, 1902, the League held its first public meeting in a committee room of the West Didsbury Public Hall, Burton Road. It was hoped to prevail on some well-known local figure to take the chair, but there was no rush on the part of those approached to accept the assignment. Mr. William Grinnell of Withington Hall, Cotton Lane, replying to the invitation, wrote that he could not possibly comply with the committee's courteous request. Mr. G. H. Gaddum, of Adria House, said that he did not think the district was ripe for amalgamation. Mr. James Heald, of Didsbury Park, replied, rather curtly, that he was strongly opposed to any amalgamation with Manchester and therefore did not need to say any more, while Lord Egerton of Tatton regretted that at such short notice he could not express any opinion on the question. In the event Thomas Eggington had to take the chair himself.

Yet like so many other movements born into ridicule the Amalgamation League eventually had its way.

133

On 14th November, 1902, only a few months after its foundation, an invitation was received from the Urban District Council to send a deputation to its General Purposes Committee. So it was that on 11th December the Council resolved to appoint a committee to go into the whole question of amalgamation with Manchester. During the autumn of 1903 the Council consented to Manchester Corporation including a clause in the Manchester Corporation (General Powers) Bill, 1904, to incorporate the Urban District within the City boundaries. This arrangement was, however, made on the understanding that the Urban District Council would seek the approval of its ratepayers by taking a poll and that the scheme would be dropped should the poll be unfavourable.

The poll took place on 26th January, 1904. The ratepayers voted by marking cards sent to them by the Council. When the cards were sorted and counted it was found that 4,086 votes had been cast in favour of the proposal, 805 against, and 48 in favour subject to the condition that secondary schools were provided.

Amalgamation with Manchester became a fact at midnight on 8th November, 1904. Thus Didsbury found itself under the fourth Local Authority it had known in a period of less than thirty years. Part of the arrangement was that for ten years local affairs were to be managed by a special committee of Manchester Corporation, the Withington Committee, composed of the councillors and aldermen for the district, which still retained its headquarters at the old town hall in Lapwing Lane. This part of the scheme was reconsidered at the end of the ten years and discontinued. The six wards of the old Urban District became three wards of the City, Withington, Didsbury, and Chorlton-cum-Hardy, each with three councillors and one alderman. The first councillors elected for Didsbury were Messrs. Fletcher Moss, C. K. Mayor and C. F. Edwards. Mr. W. E. Harwood, the vice-chairman of the then defunct Urban District Council was selected as the alderman, much to the annoyance of Fletcher Moss who considered that he had a greater claim to the honour. Writing about the matter, many years later, he rather immodestly proclaimed that he was the historian of Didsbury who had made its name known all over the world! Possibly in order to console himself for his disappointment he claimed all the credit for the amalgamation for himself. In his own account of the matter he did not once mention the Amalgamation League. This omission may have been by way of revenge, for despite its difficulty in finding chairmen for its meetings the League never approached him; nor did he receive the slightest mention in the copious records of its affairs which it preserved.

Building operations were suspended in Didsbury and elsewhere during the First World War, but after the armistice Manchester Corporation conceived the idea of building a completely new road linking Rusholme with East Didsbury, to cope with the ever-increasing volume of traffic. Kingsway was declared open on 11th April, 1923, but at that time it went no further than Parrs Wood. The houses on either side of it were built in the late 1920's and early 1930's.

In 1924 part of the land on the north side of Fog Lane, which had belonged to the trustees of Audenshaw School in the eighteenth century, was purchased by Wallace Cranmer James Fleeson, after whom Cranmer Road was named. All the houses in that neighbourhood were built at about that time. Those in the vicinity of Didsbury Park and Ruabon Road were built in 1925 by Didsbury Park Estate Ltd.

The stretch of Kingsway between Parrs Wood and the river, which crossed Boathouse Farm and Broad Oak Farm, was opened in 1933 and the housing estates fronting to it, and also fronting to Parrs Wood Road were built during the following year. At the same time the remnant of the Ford Bank estate was purchased by Ford Bank Estate Ltd. from Herbert Levinstein, a Doctor of Chemistry, who had been instrumental in the development of poison gases during the war. The old mansion house was demolished and the present houses erected.

And so we come to the present day. What changes there have been! Didsbury is a different place indeed from the village from which William de Didsbury drove his oxen to the common pasture and through which the armies of Prince Rupert, Sir William Brereton and the Young Pretender tramped. Thomas Wood would not recognise it today; scarcely indeed would Fletcher Moss! The spring in Stenner Lane has dried up; there is almost no trace of Northenden Ford and the old road to Gatley, down Millgate Lane, is overgrown with weeds. Didsbury is in danger of losing its identity. It is fortunate indeed that in recent years a group of citizens, who love the district they live in, have come together to form the Didsbury Civic Society, to ensure that the amenities of the area are preserved and extended and, at the same time, to revive an interest in the fascinations of its past. May their efforts meet with the success they so well deserve. May they move from strength to strength.

INDEX

INDEX

139

140